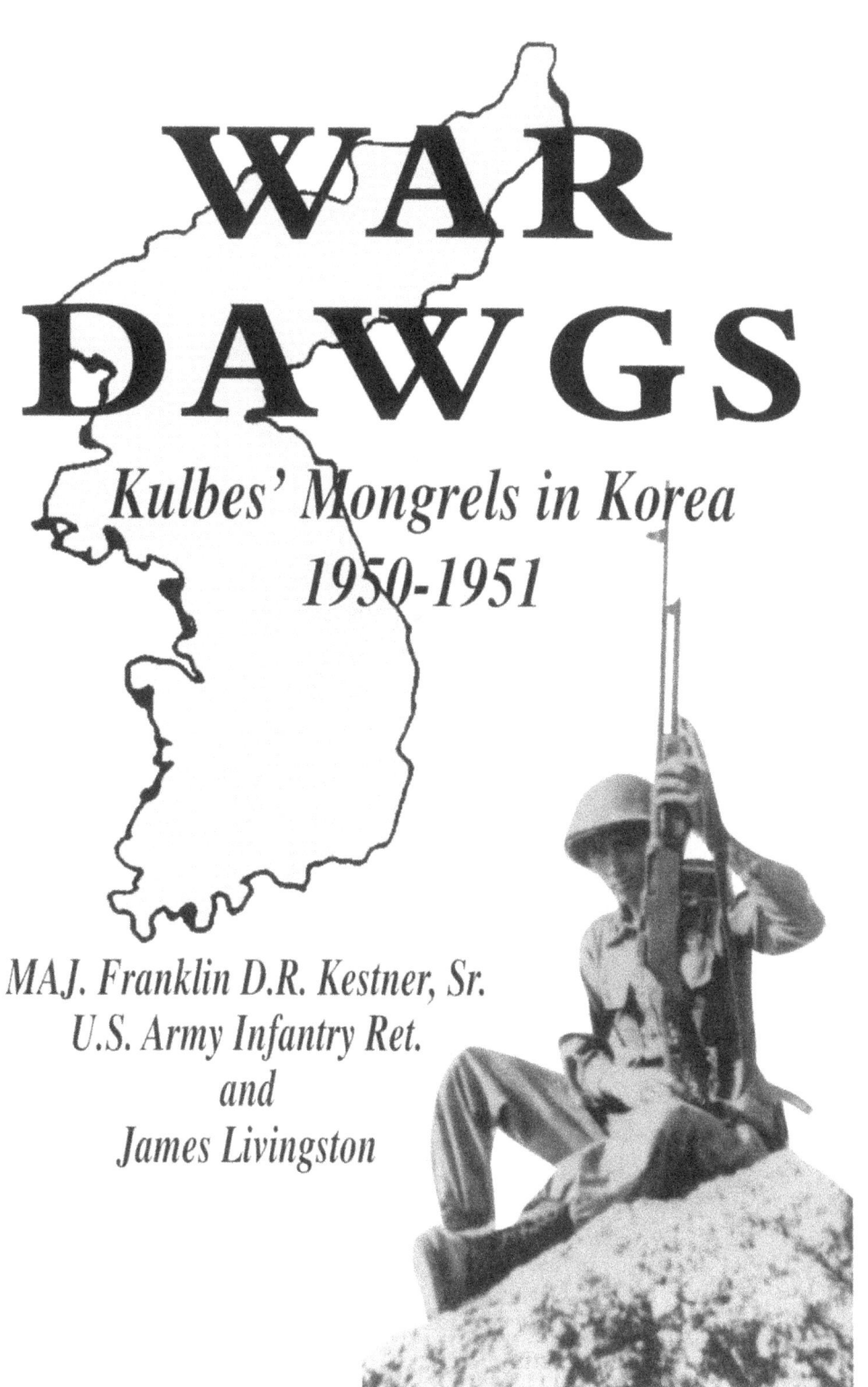

WAR DAWGS

Kulbes' Mongrels in Korea 1950-1951

MAJ. Franklin D.R. Kestner, Sr.
U.S. Army Infantry Ret.
and
James Livingston

TURNER PUBLISHING COMPANY

TURNER PUBLISHING COMPANY
412 Broadway • P.O. Box 3101
Paducah, Kentucky 42002 - 3101
(502) 443-0121

Copyright © 1998 Franklin D. R. Kestner, Sr.
and James Livingston
Publishing Rights: Turner Publishing Company
This book or any part thereof may not be
reproduced without the written consent of the
author and publisher.

Turner Publishing Company Staff:
Editor: Bill Schiller
Designer: Shelley R. Davidson

Library of Congress Catalog
Card No. 98-60840
ISBN: 978-1-56311-451-9

Additional copies may be purchased directly
from the publisher. Limited Edition.

Photos Provided Courtesy of:
Leland Lipscomb, Larry Lindgren, Thomas
Ortega, and Bob Henley.

TABLE OF CONTENTS

	Dedication	4
	Prologue	6
Chapter 1:	First Command	8
Chapter 2:	First Combat	19
Chapter 3:	In a Village, Nameless to Protect the Guilty	21
Chapter 4:	South of the Han	27
Chapter 5:	Black Water, Black Sky	32
Chapter 6:	The Cruelest Month	36
Chapter 7:	Crossing the Same River Twice	42
Chapter 8:	East of Wonju	48
Chapter 9:	Combat Stripes	54
Chapter 10:	Johnny	59
Chapter 11:	The Dark on Me	62
Chapter 12:	HighTower	71
Chapter 13:	The Peace Treaty with Japan	88
Chapter 14:	In Trouble with the Draft Board	96
Chapter 15:	The Church of the Haunting	106
Chapter 16:	Pyongyang Sue	110
Chapter 17:	A Note About Infantry Tactics	116
Chapter 18:	Bull Dog Six, Out!	122
Chapter 19:	Thanks to Mrs. Eleanor	127
Chapter 20:	What's Gonna Happen When We Get Home?	135
Chapter 21:	The More Things Change	143
Chapter 22:	Meals, Wheels, and Dollar Bills	152
	War Dawg Epilogue	156
	Acknowledgements	160

DEDICATION

This book is dedicated to all my teachers in Kulbes' Mongrels, especially Lieutenant Colonel Kulbes', Sergeant Morton, Colonel Rosen, and Major Smith, who taught me leadership and Cornelius Vanderstilt, who taught me faith.

Captain Philip A. Kulbes, Company Commander Company D 10th Engineer (C) Bn.3rd Inf. Div. Korea 1950 - 1951.

1/Lt. Norman R. Rosen, 3rd Plt. Leader, 1950 - 1951.

SFC Cornelius Vandersteldt, 2nd Platoon Co. D 10th Engrs (C) Battalion, Korea 1951 - 1952.

1/Lt. Geroge E. Smith, 2nd Plt. Leader 1950 - 1951.

17 year old Private Frank Kestner.

Prologue

This is the second book in an ongoing trilogy about the military career of a remarkable soldier and officer. The first book, "To the Last Man!" Kulbes' Mongrels at the Chosin Reservoir, described D Company of the 10th Combat Engineers during the icy ordeal at the Chosin Reservoir and their against-all-odds withdrawal to Pusan.

During the month of November, 1950, 350,000 Chinese troops quietly joined forces with a nearly defeated North Korean People's Army. On November 28, the two armies initiated a surprise counter-attack against combined South Korean, American, and United Nations' forces so confident of victory that their northern advance had been labeled the "Home By Christmas Offensive." The undetected build-up of forces in those snowy peaks and canyons was a remarkable military feat. Equally remarkable was the subsequent defense and evacuation from Hungnam to Pusan by the 7th and 5th Marines, to which Kulbes' Mongrels had been temporarily attached.

That story was told from the point of view of seventeen- year-old Private Frank Kestner. He was weeks away from basic training, and mere months away from his childhood in what is called the "Boot Heel" section of southeastern Missouri.

The battles at the Chosin, where he was roughly introduced to combat, have been named among the most savage in military history. D Company was awarded a Presidential Unit Citation for its role in that devastating combat. Company commander Captain Kulbes was personally nominated for a Congressional Medal of Honor.

By the time the Mongrels arrived at Hamhung, inside the perimeter held by General Soule's Third Division, they had suffered more than 50% casualties. Their daily reports had been lost in the chaos of battle, however, and for too long, they were not recognized for their role at the Chosin. Their status as a temporarily "lost" company, combined with their cocky attitude, created ongoing friction with headquarters. As a result, they were assigned to demolition of docks and ordnance and had to watch as units they had fought alongside debarked for the security of Pusan. In reality, that assignment was probably both a punishment for their cocky attitude as well as recognition of their notable efficiency as combat engineers. "War Dawgs" was General Soule's nickname for the Mongrels.

It was only when he had arrived at the secure perimeter of Pusan, with the horror of the Chosin already behind him, that young Kestner learned the battalion Chaplain had arranged for him to be sent home. The Chaplain's kind intentions were in response to a policy initiated by Eleanor Roosevelt to return all soldiers under the age of eighteen back to the States. Private Kestner was dedicated to D Company, however, and he found a loophole: he had turned eighteen by the time the orders arrived. He carried his case up the chain of command, finally pleading with the commanding Colonel at Battalion, who countermanded the orders, permitting his return to the Mongrels. He returned to his company with the promotion of Pfc. and was also made assistant squad leader of 1st Squad.
—James Livingston

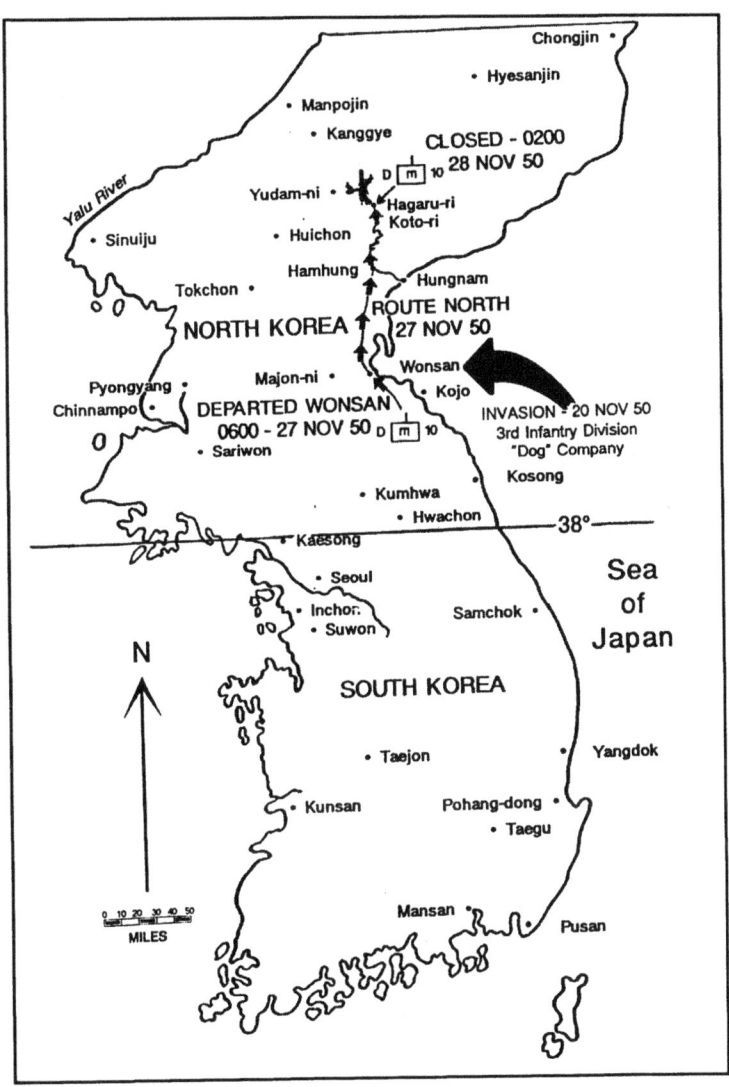

Chapter 1:

FIRST COMMAND

I was young, immortal and I liked war. I know it's not politically correct to admit that, but in war, you know exactly who your friends are and who your enemies are. You don't have to act like you don't know the difference.

On January 2nd, 1951, Kulbes' Mongrels were still at Pusan (the Southern tip of Korea) waiting to start north toward Seoul where the Eighth Army was under massive assault. For nearly a week, we had rested and received reinforcements. In a few days, we would return to combat.

I woke in darkness, lit a lantern and dressed. Before leaving for chow, I pushed my M1919 bayonet inside my boot. It was my lifesaver on East Hill, up at the Chosin, and I liked to keep it handy.

Overnight snow had frosted the ground, and there was a thin veneer of ice floating in the slow eddies of the stream beside Dog Company's bivouac. I looked down at the new stripe on my sleeve. I was a Private First Class and assistant squad leader of First Squad, Second Platoon, Company D of the 10th Combat Engineers. We called ourselves Kulbes Mongrels, after our commander, Captain Kulbes. I was the only member of 1st Squad who made it back from the Chosin, so I was the assistant squad leader to nobody.

On my way to chow, I saw that first squad's bullet-riddled two and a half ton truck (D-21), had a large whitewashed "X" on the passenger's windshield, marking her for the scrap heap. That would be the work of the new motor sergeant. I added his name to the list. The Chinese and North Koreans were first on the list. Next, Harry Truman, followed by all members of the U.S. Congress (both houses). Finally, any one else who was uppity, lazy, or lax. The new motor sergeant fit right in.

The mess sergeant said we had fresh eggs, bacon, hot biscuits and home-made

Matthew Bunker Ridgway, General, United States Army.

milk gravy. I asked for four eggs and four slices of bacon, a double portion of biscuits and gravy, coffee with milk and lots of sugar. After the Chosin, I was down from a hundred, fifty-five to a hundred, thirty-five. Eating on the run will do that to you. I was sopping the last bit of gravy with my last biscuit when Sergeant Morton sat down across from me. "You look frazzled," he said.

"I need a haircut, I think." I'd picked up a lot of gray hair at the Chosin, and it didn't show as long as I kept it cut short. I had only turned eighteen on December 21 and already, I had the gray-flecked topnotch of a man in his forties.

"I read somewhere that it takes 43 face muscles to frown," Sarge said, "And only seven, I think, to smile."

"I need the exercise, Sarge. I'm pretty mad about D-21. The new motor sergeant has marked her for the scrap-heap."

"Does she run ok?"

"She's beat up, but she purrs, Sergeant."

"We'll check it out later. You're getting replacements this morning."

I had a second coffee with canned milk and sugar, then went back to the squad tent. Duty had been easy those last few days while we reorganized. D Company had taken more than 50% casualties when three hundred thousand or so Chinese joined the North Korean forces in late November, 1950.

It had looked for a while like Korea was going to be a Dunkirk, but General Walker had ordered the speedy evacuation of Tenth Corps from the northeast coast, at Hungnam, and incorporated them into Eighth Army, at Pusan, on the extreme southern tip of the peninsula. The remainder of Eighth Army had held a day-to-day defensive perimeter north of Seoul, with minute-by-minute plans for a scorched earth policy and immediate withdrawal south down the peninsula toward Pusan and a full-scale evacuation.

On December 23, with Eighth Army in full-scale retreat toward Seoul, General Johnnie Walker's jeep driver pulled out of line in a long, slow convoy directly into the path of an oncoming two and a half ton troop truck. A tough, savvy old warrior who mixed it up with his front-line troops, General Walker had begun his career serving under General Pershing in the border skirmishes with Pancho Villa. In fact, on one patrol, he and a young Eisenhower had been struck by the same bolt of lightning. He had fought in World War II and had been in command of Eighth Army since they debarked at Pusan, in September of 1950. It was bitter and ironic that his career would end in a traffic accident.

General Matt Ridgway assumed immediate, aggressive command. He ordered his field commanders to throw away their plans for a withdrawal and to begin planning combined offensive/defensive strategies. A few days later, when he asked one commander to see his plans for a counter-offensive, he was told there were none. The commander was relieved of duty on the spot, the first of many field commanders to be similarly relieved. Ridgway was harsh and summary, but his aggressiveness quickly changed the defeatist attitude of Eighth Army. Soldiers began to use free time to service their firearms and to sharpen bayonets. His cocky independence was soon reflected in a slogan that you could hear everywhere in Korea: "There's a right way, a wrong way, and a Ridgway."

Generals MacArthur and Ridgway (left) visiting on the line near Seoul.

On New Year's Day, the Chinese forces crossed the 38th Parallel, despite General Ridgway's wishes, and Eighth Army withdrew, but held a line maybe twenty miles south of Seoul, which was as far south as we were going to go. You had to like General Ridgway. When he had to abandon Seoul, he ripped the seat out of his pajamas and tacked it to a wall in his room with a sign:

TO THE COMMANDING GENERAL CCF:
WITH THE COMPLIMENTS OF THE
COMMANDING GENERAL, EIGHTH ARMY

I finally met the new members of first squad. Pfc. E. L. "High Pockets" Wilkinson, who'd been with Dog Company since Japan, was transferred from another squad to be our driver. While the new recruits settled in, High Pockets walked out with Sergeant Morton and me to check out D-21. High Pockets pronounced her in good mechanical condition, and Morton talked to the motor sergeant who argued that it was silly to keep an old truck when we could have a new one. Morton went to Captain Kulbes, who called the motor sergeant in and told him that he was not to scrap D-21 until further notice.

While High Pockets and Peter Talley, one of the new recruits to first squad, worked on the truck that afternoon, they counted 170 bullet holes, including the one through the driver's side windshield that killed the previous motor sergeant during our escape from Hagaru. I jawed a little with the other new recruits, but I wasn't much of a talker unless the subject was demolitions, combat construction, or infantry maneuvers. Those topics made for what I thought of as good conversation.

A Quartermaster Supply Convoy bivouacked across the stream that afternoon, and we had our last hot showers and equipment replacement for maybe a month. I had lost my duffel bag, but the man in front of me in line got the last new one. He turned in his old raggedy one, and the supply sergeant tried to hoist that off on me. I harumphed off to the mess tent and got an empty 50-lb. potato sack that would serve me just fine, thank you.

Next morning D-21 was missing. I went to chow before I looked for her and found her parked behind the squad tent. She looked as out of character as Eleanor Roosevelt dressed for the Prom. Eleanor Roosevelt was also on my list; it was a long list, back then. It was Mrs. Roosevelt's idea that nobody under eighteen be allowed to serve in Korea. That had almost gotten me shipped back home...where I didn't want to be. D-21 had new side boards, new mirrors, new seats, new wheels and tires, head lights, a new canvas top, and, inside the cab, a new weapons rack. The new items were totally incongruous with her scratches and scrapes as well as the bullet holes. About then, Talley and High Pockets sauntered around the squad tent. "The Quartermaster Corps isn't likely to miss those parts, do you think?" High Pockets asked. Nah," I answered. "But we'll keep her low just in case until we head north."

"Talley and I are going to paint her, and nobody will recognize her."

"Have you seen the new squad leader?" I asked.

"He's still at headquarters," Talley said. "He's trying to get transferred out."

"He just got here," I said.

It was another lazy day...that's what Captain Kulbes called an Equipment Maintenance and Personal Hygiene day. I was ready to move north. After the Chosin, I had a personal agenda. I napped a while, woke in time for lunch, then squeezed in another nap during the afternoon, before dinner.

We had steak and mashed potatoes, green beans and cornbread. I was giving my full attention to a slice of apple pie with coffee, when Epps slithers into the mess tent. He was a slacker and a cheat who would earn one forlorn stripe one week and lose it the following week. We had been sparring around for as long as the Dogs had been in Korea.

"Hey, Gung-Ho!" he says, to me, and to everybody in the tent. "I see they found more suckers to be in your squad."

I let it slide, focusing on the apple pie. But it's starting to get crowded inside the tent since Epps showed up. He doesn't have enough sense to stop when he's ahead, though. "Your new squad leader is the only one with any brains," Epps says. "He's transferring out."

"Work tomorrow, you guys," I say to High Pockets, Talley and another first squad recruit, Pfc. Lafonte. I return my mess kit and stop at the doorway of the tent to ask Epps if he wants to settle everything outside.

"Some other time," he says.

After chow, there's a meeting of squad leaders of 2nd Platoon. Sergeant Morton says I should attend, so I finally meet first squad's new leader. Afterwards, I hang out in Sergeant Morton's tent, where there's been a miracle. An unopened bottle of Canadian Club has materialized in his foot locker. Unscrewing the cap, he offers me a drink for about the dozenth time and for about the dozenth time I decline.

"What about your beer rations?" he asks, pouring a long gurgle of whiskey into a canteen cup half full of black coffee.

"You can have those, too."

"We're moving north in a couple of days," he says.

"I'm ready."

"Maybe too ready. You still have a grudge."

"A little."

"Remember that it's a job, kid, not a damned vendetta." He takes a sip of his drink. "This coffee must be Maxwell House," he says. "It's good to the last drop." Looking at my face, he asks, "What's wrong?"

"What's a vendetta?"

He leans forward on his cot and flicks something from my shoulder. "It's when you have a chip, right here. It makes you stand out so you're an easy target."

I walked back to the squad tent through a night as clear and crisp as the point of a bayonet. There was a silver moon and stars so bright that I could make out my breath in the air.

You could call it a vendetta, I guess. I had watched my best friend, Roby, take point-blank rounds from a Chinese burp gun at the Chosin, and I was looking forward to payback, now, when the odds were more nearly even. My temper had nearly landed me in front of Captain Kulbes, though, and I had vowed to myself that from then on, I would be unflappable. The new squad leader and I talked a while inside the tent, but I got bored in a hurry. He was a reservist who had done desk duty during World War Two and was understandably bitter about leaving a wife and two kids for a combat assignment. I could sympathize, but who wanted a whiner squad leader? I made it a point to call him Corporal.

Breakfast next day was back to normal: spam, fried with a canned pineapple ring on top; powdered eggs, and powdered, chalky milk. Fresh biscuits, though, with grape jelly. After breakfast, High Pockets fueled up and drove old D-21 around to the squad tent. She had a new coat of paint and a new name on her hood, "Gloria".

"Let me guess," I said. "Your girlfriend is named Gloria?"

"Good guess," he answered.

"Where's the squad leader?"

"He's at headquarters working on his transfer," Talley said. "He said he would be here in time to pull out."

I didn't say anything about the squad leader. See how tranquil and self-contained I was becoming? This is called personal growth.

"He's ready to go home," High Pockets said. "He's smart. Did you really turn down a chance to go home?"

"Do you have a problem with that?"

"Not really," High Pockets said. "It doesn't make a lot of sense."

"Don't pay any attention to Epps."

Talley kept his mouth shut. I could grow to like this guy.

The squad leader, bless his heart, finally worked us into his schedule, and we joined the 2nd Platoon convoy on a long drive north, to the Naktong River, where we spent ten hours repairing a pontoon bridge. We were maybe five miles from the Sea of Japan, up a wide river valley with rocky, barren banks. A cold wind whistled through the bridge rigging all day, and the snow run-off of the river splashed our boots and leggings and sleeves while we skittered on the slippery pontoons.

After work, we bathed in the stream au naturel. You had to run from the squad tent wrapped in a blanket, drop the blanket in a dry place on the bank and wade into thirty-two degree water. Splash yourself wet, lather, rinse, wrap yourself in the blanket and pick your way barefoot, teeth-chattering, and goose-pimpled, back to the space heater in the warm squad tent. Then, chow: spam again, cubed with pineapple chunks, mashed potatoes and gravy, creamed corn, fruit cocktail with white cake, and lots of coffee. Ahhh... Army Life!

There was a company formation following chow next morning. After the first sergeant called us to order, Captain Kulbes stood on the front bumper of his jeep. "Men, we are moving north tomorrow morning to join the Hong Kong Highlanders, who don't have an engineer unit. We will work long and hard on roads and bridges, and we are likely to meet the enemy. We will assume a combat posture. If you're new to combat, listen and learn from the experienced men in your unit. Take advantage of the time off you have today."

Before dawn next morning, I was rousting first squad from their gentle slumbers, the lamp swaying in a strong wind that flapped the doorway and moaned through the treetops outside. We had a quick breakfast in the company mess, then picked up a box of C-Rations apiece, for the trip. I loaded enough ammunition for a platoon into D-21, and as much as I could carry for my own personal use: four grenades, a rocket launcher and two rockets, two full cartridge belts and two bandoliers. On East Hill, at the Chosin, I learned that the sound of a firing pin clicking on an empty chamber was the loneliest, most forlorn sound in the world. At sunrise, Dog Company was ready to roll, but we didn't pull out until sunset. I heard a twelve hour roll call of sad stories that wrenched my heart. Most of the guys in first squad had not left behind mere jobs, but high-paying, brilliant careers for which they were ideally suited by talent and by psychological disposition. And there was even sadder news: some of them had to leave Karen or Sharon or Trudy or Judy behind. These were ideal matches, you understand, destined from the moment the first ray of sunshine shone on the cold and lonely earth. Somehow, I managed not to break down in bitter sobbing the whole long day. This is called personal resiliency.

For myself, there wasn't much of anything to leave behind, and besides, I liked the damned Army. When we finally got word to move out, I took my accustomed position at the tailgate of D-21. It was about 30 degrees, and wet, with wind whistling under the tarp. It was pretty thoughtless of the Army to pack us off this way. One of the new men was getting chapped lips from the wind, and another had cold feet. We drove several hours before we stopped at a thick grove of trees, safely inside the perimeter of the Highlanders.

We had a quick spot of tea, standing around diesel-drum heaters, stamping our feet and holding our hands up close to the heat. In a clipped mumble that I barely recognized as English, an older soldier with mutton-chops asked me how old I was.

"Eighteen," I conceded. I was touchy about it. "But I'm old for my age."

"You're old enough, I suppose," he said.

He asked about my home and my women. I told him I was from Missouri, and there was a girl there that I had an eye for. He told me that I talked funny.

Another Brit looked into my empty canteen cup and poured bottled water into it. I took a long swallow and my throat locked up. I bent over, coughing and spewing.

"It's gin, Yank. You have to sidle up to it most politely, the way you approach a pretty woman."

"You guys talk funny too," I said.

I saw that first squad thought I was pretty hilarious. The bottle went around the circle and one of the new recruits turned it up for a long swig. He lowered the bottle, and after a long exhalation, said, "This stuff is for men."

"Aye." the Brit said, taking a swig himself. "For men and other fools."

Morton yelled to move it! We set up camp, and the Highlanders started a large bonfire in the dead center of the perimeter that crackled and shot burning sparks twenty feet into the air. It was like a neon sign in Chinese saying, "Aim your artillery here, Old Chaps."

The Captain ordered only a limited perimeter patrol that night, and I slept another unbroken sleep, pure luxury. For the next few days, we worked on the main supply route north, widening and reinforcing the narrow Korean roads. The job required long hours of spreading river gravel with D-handled shovels over fallen trees that are wired end to end.

On my dad's birthday, January 8, I wrote a long letter home, the first one since my passage aboard the U.S.S. Freeman, from Hungnam to Pusan. First squad got a new recruit, old pipe-smoking Corporal Meters, an Army Regular in his forties, who had a son older than I was. He was a construction specialist who, like everyone in first squad except High Pockets and me, had no combat experience. Night guard duty was 10-2 and 2-6, on a rotating schedule so that everybody got a full night's sleep every third night. Daytimes, there was a screening patrol into the hills around camp, and a reinforcement-alert squad in reserve at the command post. The squad leader and I fell into a workable routine: he took care of the paper work and assigned daily duty, then stayed out of the way. On our first screening patrol, it was decided that I would take first point while he brought up the rear. We assembled the squad and walked into the brush.

"All right," I said, "You guys fan out and follow me. Standard infantry formation." I turned and picked my way toward the ridge of the hill behind camp, watching the ground in front of me for booby traps or mines, watching the hilltop for snipers. When I turned back to check the squad, they were following in single file like a school class marching to lunch.

"Lafonte!" I yelled, to the recruit immediately behind me. "What does infantry formation mean?"

"It means fan out."

"You guys got that?" I asked. "One burst from a Chinese machine-gun position and we would all be dead." We walked the rest of the way to the hilltop more or less like soldiers.

From there, we could overlook a little valley with terraced rice paddies and a couple of peasant huts. I told the squad leader that I would take Talley and Lafonte with me to check them out. The rest of the squad could spread out along the ridge and cover us.

The three of us walked down to the ridge of a slightly smaller hill, then through some trees behind the huts. I had the men cover me while I ran the last twenty or so yards to the first hut. Finding it empty, I dashed across an open space between the huts to the second, empty hut. I walked out to the paddy and signalled an all clear. There was a Chinese soldier frozen in the ice of the paddy. One down, I thought. After dinner that night, the first sergeant called us to attention and Captain Kulbes took his accustomed position on the front bumper of the jeep...the lights shining. "Men, we have a new mission. We'll remove mines and repair roads for the 64th Heavy Tank Battalion and the 65th Infantry Regiment on the fastest possible move north toward Seoul. We'll widen and stabilize the roads wherever necessary for 3rd Division artillery. We'll train infantry for crossing the Han River in assault boats. We will meet the enemy. There'll be long hours and lots of hard work, but I'll be there with you. Pack tonight."

Next morning, we'd gone about fifteen miles north, when we were stopped by a staff officer from Third Division. Second Platoon was ordered to repair a blown railroad trestle about a mile east of the main road. We dropped out of the company convoy and drove east along a crooked little ox cart trail that had been flattened by heavy traffic. We passed through a patrol kept by an infantry company from the 15th Infantry Regiment, drove down into a narrow valley, and stopped at the blown railroad bridge. There were new timbers and rails and ties strapped onto railroad flat cars shipped up by Third Division. No cranes, though. We were going to have to grunt the timbers and rails into place.

First squad had gotten another regular Army replacement, a construction specialist who was also a Sergeant. Under Sergeant Morton's close supervision, the work moved quickly. The squad leader found lots of opportunities for executive level decision-making, mainly tagging along behind Sergeant Morton, or the work might have gone even faster.

We worked through the night, eating and sleeping in shifts. By late the next afternoon, the day Wrong Way Tunnicliffe got his nickname, the locomotive chugged slowly across and back on its test run. Second Platoon cheered, picked up tools, and drove back to the main supply route, a tuckered crew of railroad hot dogs. From there we drove maybe twenty miles north before we rejoined the other Mongrels, still in time for company chow.

We were having chow when Lieutenant Tunnicliffe's jeep rattled up the road from behind us and turned into the company bivouac, a little too fast for the sharp turn. With his tires throwing gravel and small stones every which way, he skidded to a stop in front of the command post. Captain Kulbes had assigned him to drive up ahead to locate and mark the bivouac area for the night.

Third Division had advanced beyond our position, he told the Captain, and we could set up camp inside their perimeter, where there was a PX and even a movie planned for that night. Best of all, we would need only a perimeter patrol, and most of the men could sleep.

"Come with me," the Captain said. When they were outside the tent, he asked Lieutenant Tunnicliffe to point out the direction of Third Division. When Tunnicliffe pointed, Captain Kulbes said that was south. We were moving north. "We've already moved camp," he said. "You probably didn't notice because it was dark when you got back. Go have dinner."

First squad drew a second screening patrol a few days later. We tramped the hillsides without incident, then had a picnic lunch of C-rations on a sunny peak and gazed at the snowy back-bone of peaks of the central mountain ranges. That afternoon, we had uneventfully completed the remainder of a large perimeter. It was like boy scouts playing army. When we returned to camp at the end of the day, the squad leader caught up with me.

"Is this necessary, do you think?" he asked.

"What?"

"This elaborate patrol. I wonder if we need to cover as much ground as we did today."

"It's orders," I said.

"A couple of the squads just walk out into the woods and relax."

"You're joking."

"No."

I looked behind us to make sure we were out of hearing of the rest of the squad. "Did you report them to Sergeant Morton?"

"I'm not going to rat on them," he said.

"It's not ratting," I said. "The security of the whole company is at stake."

"Look around, Kestner. We're miles behind the combat line."

"It's orders. If you want to take up policy with Sergeant Morton, go ahead."

"Are you going to tell him?"

"Damn right."

"I'm not suggesting that first squad slack off," the Corporal said. "But I don't think we should rat."

"We have orders," I said.

Next morning, first squad was assigned mine-removal ahead of the 64th Heavy Tank Battalion, away from camp, where some hot-under-the-collar Pfc. Kestner might talk too much. Captain Kulbes already knew about the slacker squads and didn't want them to get wind of the trap he had set. At chow that night, the Mongrels were two squads short. They were at Division, awaiting courts-martial.

From the front bumper of his jeep, the Captain explained in great detail what constituted dereliction of duty and its penalties. Dishonorable Discharge was the slightest penalty and would not be applied again in Dog Company. Another such incident would call for imprisonment. Dereliction of duty under fire called for either life-imprisonment or a firing-squad, depending on the severity of the crime.

There was no chatter in Dog Company that night, and at sack-time, I slid into my bag in unaccustomed silence. I could hear each flap of canvas in the night wind, a jeep passing on the main road, the sound of my own breathing. I thought about home.

I wondered what it would feel like to get a letter from the Army saying your son had been sentenced to twenty years' hard labor or executed by firing squad. I began to wonder how the Army had the power to execute a soldier. Did it begin with somebody who had been drafted and didn't want to serve in the first place? Who does a person belong to? How could a democracy force people to go to war and kill them if they didn't do as they were told? I finally drifted into a claustrophobic dream that I thought I had forgotten.

I'm running, and I can't remember a time when I wasn't running, but I'm not tired. The thing chasing me is like a dog, but it's more than a dog. If I turn to look, it will kill me and eat my body.

There's water in front of me. If I can cross the water and get into the thick bushes on the other side, I may be able to escape. The water is muddy and it churns with water moccasins. The air is clammy with the stench of venom. I stand for a moment on the bank, feeling the hot breath of the dog on my neck. If I turned to face him, there would be only darkness.

I start to turn, but the mud under my feet gives way and I slide down the bank, into the silent water.

"Kestner!" I was in the dark squad tent and the Corporal was shaking my foot. It was my turn to stand guard.

Chapter 2:

First Combat

I signal to halt, and crouch low on the ridge, but there's scant cover. I crawl toward a small outcropping of crumbly rock, raise the barrel of my M-1, and draw a bead on a North Korean soldier. He is eating rice with his fingers on a windy hilltop and does not know that his life is nearly over. Behind me, a voice in first squad asks what is happening and another voice says to keep it quiet. It's the ten damn stooges on patrol.

I crawl backwards, downhill. "There are four or five North Koreans up top," I whisper to the Corporal when I'm below the ridge. "We'll take them as prisoners. I'll go with Talley and High-Pockets around to the right. Take a couple of men up into those trees and cover us. The rest of the squad can cover from here. Nobody fires a shot unless I give the command. Fix bayonets, you guys."

The three of us walked downhill a few yards and picked our way across a steep slope of icy snow and slippery stones. When we were below the enemy, we spread out and waited for the Corporal's fire team to take their positions. We then began carefully crawling up the slope.

Within minutes, everyone was in position. I fired a round into the rocks behind the soldiers and yelled, "Surrender!"

Instantly, they jumped to their feet and raised their hands into the air. "GI number one," they pleaded. "No shoot! No shoot!"

"Just wait!" I yelled to Talley who had stood up, ready to advance. "Keep them covered."

I slid downhill on my butt and approached from their rear. When I nudged one of the Koreans onto his knees with the side of my bayonet, the three others quickly did the same.

"OK," I yelled, covering the prisoners until Talley and High Pockets arrived. After I signaled to the Corporal to approach, I searched each prisoner slowly and methodically. Not one of them had a wallet or identification. I found a few North Korean coins in one man's pocket, which I kept. In the jacket pocket of the last man I searched, I found a Brownie snapshot of an old woman who looked like she might be his grandmother. He squirmed, wanting to reach for the photograph. I turned it over to look at the blank backside. I returned the photo to his pocket, and he bowed his head ever so slightly forward in gratitude.

By the time the Corporal's team advanced, I could breathe again. First squad met the enemy without casualty and had taken four prisoners of war. Never mind that these particular Korean soldiers seemed a pathetic group of left-behind outcasts clad in grease-stained, camp-fire scorched winter quilting. Never mind that they only had two rifles and a handful of bullets among them. First squad passed its first combat challenge.

Chapter 3:

IN A VILLAGE, NAMELESS TO PROTECT THE GUILTY

It was late as we pulled into a railroad station a few miles northwest of Taejon. Before we even climbed from the trucks, Sergeant Morton said we should immediately assume combat posture. Chinese forces had broken through Eighth Army's line (six miles north) and were following the railroad due south.

We set up machine gun outposts every three hundred yards, each one linked to command headquarters by direct phone line. By great bad luck, Sergeant Morton assigned Bomler, from second squad, to join me in the first outpost, maybe a quarter of a mile up the railroad tracks north of the station. Other machine gun emplacements would form a large horseshoe-shaped perimeter from there.

Lieutenant Smith wanted experienced men at the first outpost, and Bomler and I had come through the Chosin more or less whole and sane. I say more or less: I had built a mental bunker with no admittance from outside. I don't know what happened inside Bomler. He was courageous and straight forward, but trigger-quick, and sometimes you had to repeat what you said to him.

We followed the train tracks to our position, almost as much by feel as by sight. Dark, low clouds threatened snow, and we were on a strict lights out. We set up about twenty yards to one side of the rails where some boulders gave us a little protection and went back to unroll the phone line. That done, we made contact with the command post and settled in.

I didn't think we had enough ammunition and told Bomler to go back for more. "We have plenty," he said. At Pusan, he'd won his Pfc. stripe back for the second or third time and wasn't about to take orders from me. "You can go, if you want," he said. "But you'll have to carry it back tomorrow morning, too."

"I'll come back through these trees, here, ok? I'll whistle."

"What?"

"I'll whistle. Don't shoot me."

Who knows why we do what we do? For some reason, I crossed to the side of the tracks opposite our position on my way back from headquarters. I whistled, and then, as if by instinct, without making a conscious decision, I crouched low behind the railway embankment.

Machine gun rounds hammered into the railroad ties and cracked against the rails above my head. The armor-piercing rounds tore up the rails. Ammo ricocheted into the woods behind me, thwacking into trees near the second machine gun emplacement. If they began to return fire, I was hash.

"Bomler!" I yelled.

There was no answer, but at least he didn't fire at me.

"Bomler, you're an idiot!"

"You're coming from the wrong direction, Kestner."

"If you're through shooting at me, I'm coming up there, ok? Don't shoot!"

I reached the machine gun alive. Bomler had gotten himself turned around in the dark and was facing toward headquarters. Sergeant Morton and Lieutenant Smith showed up almost as soon as I did. "What happened?" Lieutenant Smith asked, calm and unruffled. Nobody had been shooting at him.

Major General Robert H. Soule.

"Put somebody else up here with me," I said. "Bomler's nuts."

"I heard somebody walking along the train tracks whistling," Bomler said defensively.

"Didn't you have a prearranged signal?" asked Lieutenant Smith.

"Yeah," I said. "I was supposed to whistle."

"Do you know that you've given away our position?" the lieutenant confronted Bomler. "Let me take your M-1, and you go back with Sergeant Morton to cool down for a while. Kestner, I'll send you a replacement."

"I won't shoot at him either, sir."

I was glad to see Talley, when they sent him up. He hung close, and watched. He didn't whine. He could tell North from South.

At dawn next morning, we could hear the crash as two battalions of Third Division's 15th Regiment engaged the enemy. Briefly. In little time at all, the enemy unit was no longer what they call "viable." But even before the battle was over, Bomler had been in front of the old man, had lost his new stripe, and was peeling them spuds, scrubbing them pans.

It was an Equipment Maintenance and Personal Hygiene day, the first for a while, and overdue. I washed underwear and a pair of fatigues in my helmet and hung them to dry on a rope tied between first and second squad's tents, then turned in for a snooze. That's when Wrong Way Tunnicliffe got his second alias – Pink.

Captain Kulbes had salvaged a five gallon tin from the company mess. He removed the lid with something of a speedy can opener...a detonating cord that burned through the metal and left a smooth, rounded edge, so he could use the tin for laundry.

Lieutenant Tunnicliffe borrowed the tin for his own laundry, starting with his underwear. This included a pair of red long-johns sent from home, which dyed everything in his first load. When I woke from my nap and went to lunch, there was the prettiest little row of pink undies hanging beside First Platoon's headquarters tent.

At the line, bombs dropped and artillery hammered. We started north the next morning, and had gone only a mile or so when the convoy halted in a long, narrow valley that the Chinese had used for a staging area. There were burned-out tanks and bomb craters and a number of 500-pound bombs that had landed without exploding. Lieutenant Smith ordered me to take two men, locate all the defective bombs, and neutralize them.

I guessed that if they didn't explode when they were dropped, maybe they wouldn't explode when they were towed. We found eleven of them, tied them one at a time to the rear bumper of D-21, and pulled them into a small open area with wooded hills on three sides. I set a satchel with plastic explosives on each bomb while High Pockets drove off in D-21 to have the MPs set up road blocks three-fourths of a mile in each direction.

Talley scouted the area and found a company of the 15th Infantry Regiment camped on the hill above the bombs. An infantry Captain walked down to check it out for himself. "What's the story, Private?" he asked.

"I have to neutralize these bombs, sir. They're duds."

"If they're duds, what's the problem?"

"They can still explode, sir. They have defective fuses. I'm going to blow them in place, and I'm going to be at least a half mile away."

"But we're all dug in on the hill."

"Sir, I'm going to set off 5500 pounds of TNT. I'd really appreciate it if you would move your men at least half a mile down the backside of the hill. The MPs are going to stop road traffic for three-fourths of a mile in both directions."

"All right. I'll have the men move."

"Sir, I'll be ready to set these things off as soon as everybody is clear." I installed an electric detonator to each satchel charge and unrolled a half-mile of electric detonating line. High Pockets and Talley drove to the north road-block and waited.

The infantry Captain rejoined me. His men had moved and were secure, he said.

"Do you want to wait at the road-block, sir?"

"I'm fine," he said.

When the bombs exploded, I could see the shock wave coming. "Get down, sir," I yelled, and we both dove flat onto the road. The shock wave hit with a roar and scooted both of us, tumbling, along the ground. Dirt and rocks and tree branches crashed into the field a hundred yards away.

The Captain rolled over and began dusting himself off.

"Are you ok, sir?"

"I'm fine, private."

He walked with me back to the bomb site, where there was a deep crater a hundred and fifty feet across. The three surrounding hillsides were as stark as a plucked chickens. Traffic began to move on the road again, and an infantry Colonel stopped his jeep and walked over. "Who set that off?" he asked the Captain.

"The engineer here..." the Captain said. "He detonated a bunch of 500 pound bombs."

"They were a hazard, sir," I explained. "I was ordered to neutralize them."

"Are you the one who ordered the road block?" he asked.

"Yes sir."

"Do you like making big bangs, soldier?"

"I guess I do, sir."

"Well, you're noisy as hell, but you seem to do a thorough job of it."

About once a week, each squad would take its turn training the infantry in assault boat maneuvers for river crossings. We'd assemble in a vacant field and break up into units, three engineers per infantry squad. We would remove the assault boat from the battalion truck, load infantry equipment, and carry the boat a hundred yards into the field, double-time. There, we boarded in sequence: one engineer on each side at the bow; then, four infantrymen on each side; the equipment, more or less in the center of the boat; two more infantrymen on each side; and, finally, one engineer as boatswain. Every time we boarded, some wise rifleman would begin frantically paddling.

Safely across the river, we would debark in reverse order, and remove the equipment. Then, we'd repeat the procedure and carry the boats back to the truck.

We were close to the line, and the daily screening patrols often met enemy units. They usually threw down their weapons and surrendered at the first opportunity, but there were occasional skirmishes. With such practice, first squad was becoming a cohesive fighting unit. We were now moving in a proper infantry wedge, with the squad leader bringing up one of the two points.

On patrol near Sin Gal Li, we found a small village occupied by enemy troops. Almost automatically, the squad leader led his unit to cover the flank on our left. I assigned two men to cover the right flank, a sergeant who had been in first squad for only a few days, and a private who had been with us since Pusan.

We moved closer to the village and I challenged a North Korean soldier with a round. The other soldiers in the village surrendered almost before he hit the ground. The squad leader's unit closed from the left flank. The sergeant I had assigned to the right flank didn't show up, though, and I sent Talley to check on him while we searched the prisoners. There were twenty of them, all under-fed, under-equipped, and under-motivated.

The new sergeant is sitting down over there," Talley said, when he returned. "He's crying, and he says he's going to die."

"Really?"

"He's cracked up, I think."

When the first (and only) shot was fired, the sergeant had thrown his M-1 away and removed his weapon belt and sat on the ground, hunched-over, holding his hands to his eyes. I walked back with Talley and found the private standing vacantly beside the sergeant. "Do you have a problem?" I asked.

"It's the sergeant. He won't move."

I told Talley and the private to drag the sergeant back to the squad and to bring up the rear so that the prisoners didn't see him. The squad leader, who was more sympathetic than I, walked with him back to camp while I led the prisoners.

We delivered him to the medics, where he sat on a cot, blubbery with snot and tears and dirt, moaning again and again that he knew he was going to die. I couldn't understand it at all.

By then, Eighth Army had retaken Seoul, with its two airports. We began to see Air Force F-86s on their way north, to MIG alley, to fight Russian pilots in Russian airplanes. When MIGs were shot down and Russian pilots taken prisoners, it turns out they were all volunteers.

The Air Force bombers and troop support airplanes joined the Marine and Navy flights in devastating the Communist ground forces north of the Han River. With Seoul in hand, the next major push would be across the Han, and up toward the Iron Triangle, which was a major staging area for the Communist forces. First, the Seoul line would be solidified. We worked long days maintaining roads for the enormous traffic.

It was after a long monotonous shift on the dumb end of a D-handled shovel that High Pockets and Elliot hatched one of their brainstorms and surrounded me in my cot. "Kestner, are you ready for some excitement?" High Pockets asked.

"What kind of excitement?" Knowing the two of them, I was pretty sure that it hadn't been assigned by Lieutenant Smith.

"You have some explosives, right?" Elliot asked.

"Yeah."

"We've found a safe. It's inside a masonry building that was the village bank or something."

"Take a crow bar and a hammer. I'll come visit you in jail."

"It's a big safe," High Pockets said. "We need explosives. It's nearly dark. Nobody will ever know."

"It's probably Korean money anyway," I said. "You'll never be able to spend it." It occurred to me that I had never blown a safe and it did seem a challenge. So, I pulled a block of Composition C-3, some fuse, and a tin box of blasting caps from my gunny sack.

When we walked out to the truck, High Pockets leaned his head down to Elliot's and my height. "Peasants don't use money very much," he said, and leered. "They like gold."

It was late twilight when we got to the village. The building was the largest in town, with an arched entry and an ornately tiled roof. Two large stone dragons stood guard at the front door. Inside was a large central room and, in the back corner, a chest-high safe, packed full of treasure.

The door of the safe had a 3/8 inch crack all around it. "Detonating cord might work," I said.

"Let's use Composition C-3," Elliot said. "We don't want to be here too long in case someone shows up."

I rolled out some C-3 and worked it into the crack. I inserted a detonating cap and cut a three-minute fuse. "OK, you guys, get out of here," I said, and lit the fuse.

We hurried out front, stood behind the truck, and watched. There was a crash of orange and black thunder inside the building. The front door slammed open, then leaned forward on one hinge. The roof lifted straight up, maybe a foot, then slammed back down into place, a little bit cockeyed, but still in one piece. Broken tiles slid over the eaves and cracked onto the ground. Finally, smoke and dust and a million pieces of shredded paper began to float out the door. We dashed in to claim our treasure.

"Damn!" Elliot said, and spat a shred of paper from his lips. The safe was in ragged pieces and there was confetti floating through every square inch of the room: birth certificates, land titles... who knows?

"There goes a thousand years of history," High Pockets said.

Chapter 4:

SOUTH OF THE HAN

There were two interconnected lines of communication among the enlisted men of Dog Company: the mess tent and the company drivers. Without the drivers, we would have had no way of knowing what the officers were up to. Without the mess tent, that knowledge would have remained the independent possession of each driver. High Pockets and the mess sergeant formed the hub of this vital network.

A country kid, High Pockets was used to independent reconnaissance and scavenging around the countryside. It was predictable that in Korea, he was always turning up with unlikely information and unusual paraphernalia, odd weapons and machinery, old motors that he'd mess with until he got them running. Once, he put a burned-out Chinese troop truck back together by savaging parts from a number of other hulks. He even got it running, and we used it as an extra company vehicle. The mess sergeant was a marathon talker from Chicago whose primary mission in life was to know something before anyone else. This enabled him to be first to inform others. Almost everything that was worth knowing, and a lot of things that weren't, had a point of origin with one or both of them.

It was no accident that Captain Kulbes, who always seemed to know exactly what was going on in his company, regularly pitched his tent next door to the company mess, where he could eavesdrop. And it was no accident that Lieutenant Smith pulled High Pockets, Elliot, and me aside the morning after we had blasted a village history to shreds.

"I hear we have safe-crackers in my platoon," he said.

I was looking closely at the ground and hoping that High Pockets would live through this so I could kill him.

"That's a chargeable offense," the lieutenant said after a long sad moment. I counted how many days that I had my Pfc. stripe and wondered how long it would be, if ever, until I got another. "Since nobody got rich, I'm going to forget it," the lieutenant said. "But I strongly suggest that we don't crack any safes in the future."

First squad was on reinforcement alert that day, and only a few minutes after our career counseling session with Lieutenant Smith, a call came in from the screening patrol. They had been pinned down by a machine gun emplacement. We loaded up. We had recently traded a light machine gun to an infantry unit for a Browning

Automatic Rifle, which became a permanent addition to our arsenal. The man who carried the BAR also carried a full complement of 20-round clips. Two others would carry as much M-1 ammunition as they could, in bandoliers and field packs.

It was standard that every man on patrol carry two grenades. In my unit everybody carried four. I usually carried six grenades. I always had at least four half-pound blocks of TNT and five feet of fuse, my M-1 and 300 rounds of ammunition, four bandoliers, and my cartridge belt, full. I had 7 rounds in the rifle M-1 clip and one in chamber. Loaded and ready, we quick-timed into the brush. Lieutenant Rosen's third platoon, which hadn't left for their work assignment, dismounted from their trucks and assembled to follow.

The patrol was pinned down on the side of a hill no more than a thousand yards from camp. I took Talley and Lafonte with me up a wash and came around behind the emplacement. Twenty rounds from the automatic rifle and the engagement was over. The third platoon arrived, established a large perimeter, and set about securing the area.

I figured we did AOK, but Lieutenant Rosen had managed to redirect a whole platoon and arrive ready for combat only a few minutes later than we had. First squad still had a lot to learn. I knew we had been lucky so far, meeting only ragamuffin units stranded behind the line. The further north we got, the more that was going to change.

We moved that night to a small village on a joint operation with a South Korean artillery unit. "Bug-out" is a term that was invented during the early phases of the Korean War to describe the flight of South Korean units in combat. But they were often poorly-equipped, under-armed, and not well coordinated with the United Nations forces. Early on in his command, General Ridgway met with President Syngman Rhee, suggesting that the Korean Army needed a shake-down and reorganization, starting from the top. For his part, he began to give the South Koreans assignments where they would interlink with UN forces. As command improved, their performance improved. I know that the unit we served with set up in a strictly professional combat formation, with netting to conceal the guns, and an orderly perimeter patrol.

First squad was assigned to a joint patrol with a South Korean infantry unit early next morning. They took captive a North Korean infiltrator that we would have mistakenly let pass. He was wearing peasant clothes and carried a bundle of possessions like any other South Korean refugee, as far as I could tell.

They interrogated him and quickly learned the location of an enemy battalion. They may have used a different method of interrogation than we did...a methodology likely contradictory to the full accordances of the Geneva Convention. I don't know. I knew it was their country that was being reduced to rubble. Those were their families and friends walking south alongside the roads, with all their remaining possessions in carts and bundles.

Our two squads quickly reinforced. Second and third platoons of the engineers would provide cover for an enlarged company of South Korean infantry. By early that afternoon, we had located and taken covered positions around the enemy forces. There followed a brief artillery barrage into the canyon, and then an unsophisticated full frontal assault by the South Koreans.

In less than five minutes, the remaining enemy forces surrendered. Dog Company never fired a shot. I'm not saying that the Republic of Korea army didn't abide by the Geneva Convention, but the five-hundred-plus living men of the Consolidated Chinese Forces were methodically and quickly reduced to two hundred, still breathing, prisoners.

It was the Mongrels' first large-scale engagement and our first experience of what would become a basic pattern of confrontation. Chinese strategy was to throw enormous numbers of men at us. Our strategy was to kill as many as possible with superior fire-power.

During approximately three years, the Korean War would recapitulate the whole history of combat, from its earliest, most primitive form of horde warfare up to and including what would become a staple of the Cold War, nuclear brinksmanship. When he first assumed command, with Eighth Army reeling from the Communist New Year's Offensive, General Ridgway had to confront the possibility that the only way an evacuation at Pusan might be carried out was by using atomic bombs. For his part, General MacArthur had long wanted to enlarge the war across the Yalu, into China, provoking the Chinese and maybe the Russians, with the strong possibility of using atomic bombs. Neither possibility developed, and the conflict eventually degenerated into a stalemated World War I type of trench warfare along the 38th Parallel. The alternative was a long, ugly, and brutal ground war, but the Korean War is where the world was faced with a justifiable choice to use nuclear arms, and chose not to do so.

Because of the threat of atomic warfare, military choices during the Korean War were no longer left up to the military commanders. Instead, they were made in private phone calls between heads of state around the world, and in newspaper headlines: "Stalin Says US Must Leave Korea"; "Truman Says US To Remain." The cost of this indirect communication was paid in lives lost and a country decimated.

We continued working through an unseasonable warm spell. As snow-melt overflowed the creeks and streams, the roads grew mushy. Rice paddies thawed out. The Korean farmers kept a pit in each rice paddy where they dumped human and animal excrement alike, to make fertilizer. We called them honey holes. When it warmed up, their fragrance wafted here and there over the whole countryside.

Tank units, field artillery, and supply trucks passed in endless convoys to the Han, turning the main roads slushy. Routine road maintenance became so repetitive and dull that we looked forward to patrols and assault-boat training. One morning, we were spreading river run over a low stretch of the main supply route when I saw General Soule's jeep south of us in the long line of stop-and-go traffic. The line of traffic started, the General advanced to where we were working, and the General stopped five feet from me.

"Who's in charge here, soldier?" the general asked.

"I'm in charge right here, sir," I answered. "My commander, Captain Kulbes, is up the road."

"Are you war dawgs doing ok?"

"We're working hard, sir."

"I can see that. What do you think about how this war is going?"

"General, we need some more combat engineers to fix these roads, sir."

I immediately wished I could unsay it. I thought of something to say that would take the whiny edge out of it. But the line moved, and the jeep lurched forward. "Keep up the good work, soldier," General Soule said.

The jeep stopped about a quarter of a mile north, where Captain Kulbes was working, and the General got out. He and Captain Kulbes leaned over the hood talking for maybe ten minutes. I was pretty sure that they were deciding what to do about the complainer in first squad. Maybe 15,000 men under his command, but General Soule wanted Captain Kulbes' advice about what to do with the complainer in first squad. This is called a lack of perspective.

Snow and sleet put an end to the false spring. We relocated closer to the Han, at Kudong-no, and on the eighth of March, Lieutenant Rosen was reassigned to headquarters in Japan. Sergeant Morton stood in for the First Sergeant at morning assembly and presented the company to Captain Kulbes. From the front of his jeep, the Captain told us that Lieutenant Rosen was leaving. He began as an enlisted man and bootstrapped his way up the chain of command, eventually winning an appointment to West Point. It was because of Lieutenant Rosen as much as anybody that Dog Company had held East Hill at the Chosin. A lot of us owed our lives to him. We bid him a respectful farewell.

The Lieutenant thanked the Captain. He said that he was sorry to be the first of the original unit to leave and that he would always be proud of serving with Dog Company.

As he was leaving, Sergeant Morton called, "Company, Attention! Present Arms!" This is a command reserved for the company commander.

Captain Kulbes and Lieutenant Rosen were both surprised. Lieutenant Rosen returned Sergeant Morton's salute, and Morton sang out, "Order Arms! Parade Rest!"

"That'll be all, Sergeant," the Captain said. "Take charge of the company." Sergeant Morton called attention, saluted the Captain, and Lieutenant Rosen was gone.

He and Sergeant Morton, Captain Kulbes and Lieutenant Smith were the rock foundations of my personal Army. I modeled my performance after theirs, and my pride in the Mongrels started from the fact of their membership. I shoveled river run and tried not to think about it. It would be thirty-nine years before I saw Lieutenant Rosen again.

After Lieutenant Rosen was reassigned, his driver Bob Henley transferred into the second platoon. During our escape from Hagaru, the motor sergeant driving D-21 had been shot, and Bob had figured out in a hurry how to drive a stalled two-and-a-half ton troop truck. I rode shot gun while he scraped and gnashed between first and second gears to rejoin the convoy amid the fire of hundreds of Chinese soldiers. This was the night D-21 got most of her bullet holes.

Until Bob's transfer, most of the enlisted men survivors of the Chosin had been in first platoon: Larry Lindgren, Ray Smith, and Gene Cookus. Now, High Pockets, Bob Henley, and I formed a similar trio in the second platoon. That left Tom Ortega as the only Chosin survivor in the third platoon.

The Quartermaster set up a shower-point and clothing exchange, our first since Pusan. We stacked our arms and went into one end of the tent, stripped down, and turned in our clothes. They gave each of us a towel and small bag with soap, shampoo, tooth brushes, razors and blades. We shaved and showered and passed through to the other end of the tent, where a guy behind a long table asked us our sizes, stacked clean clothes on the table, and told us to dress outside.

My new, clean clothes had formerly belonged to Master Sergeant Wilson of the First Cavalry. For the rest of the day, every private in the company went out of his way to salute me. That night, while Bishop and High Pockets chattered about how much they were going to miss Sergeant Wilson, I removed his name tag, his First Cav patch, and all but the top, Pfc. stripe.

On March 10, we moved into the division assembly area south of the Han from where we could see Seoul and all the bombed-out bridges between. Days passed with intensified assault boat training and company drills, but we kept only a limited perimeter patrol at night and could sleep.

Chapter 5:

BLACK WATER, BLACK SKY

The light on the north bank blinked green. We clambered into the boat by twos, starting with the engineers at the bow. When the infantry squad had taken their positions, I pushed off and leaped in. At the bow, the engineers shouted commands, coordinating strokes by the infantry squad, and I steered us toward the spot where the light blinked. A howitzer round sizzled into the river upstream and detonated, sending a large wave sloshing into the boat.

After nearly a week of company drills and practice runs, we had been lulled by routine and were surprised by the order that we would cross tonight. Apparently, the enemy knew as little as we did. Artillery fire from their positions was as sporadic as it had been for the last several days, not the heavy pounding we would have received if they knew that we were delivering the 7th Regiment into their back yard. When the troops were across, we worked with C Company of the Tenth Combat Engineers building pontoon rafts to ferry the trucks and tanks. At dawn, the first units of the 64th Heavy Tank Battalion began landing north of the Han. One of the bloodiest phases of the Korean War was about to begin.

Dawn was met with enemy machine gun fire, the rapid escalation of incoming artillery, and the answering response of third division artillery from the rear. We were assigned to work with the Bridge Platoon from battalion headquarters.

The treadways are lowered into place by crane, where they are attached to the floating pontoons with a steel rod, two-and-a-half inches in diameter and four feet long, and heavy. You balance on a wet pontoon and lean out over the water, holding the rod with both hands until the anchoring devices are lined up, then pushed home. You wear a life jacket and a life-line tied around your waist. A separate line is tied to the anchoring rod in case it falls into the water. The occasional sniper fire and incoming artillery is sufficient enough to keep you from becoming too bored. It is impossible to go fast enough, but you can't go too fast, either.

Artillery thunders, the engine of the ten-ton bridging truck on the bank above you roars, and the icy snow-melt of the Han crashes against the pontoons, soaking and deafening you. Commands have to be yelled, often several times, before they are heard, and even then, you have to explain with your hands.

In the middle of it all, Epps, who has never in his life volunteered for anything, decides that he will show first squad how to build a bridge. He appears out of confusion, the rod in his hands, and leans out over the river. We struggle to align the slots on the pontoons with the slots on the treadways and yell for the rod to be inserted.

He leans still further out, then tumbles head-first into the rolling water. His safety line and the line which secures the anchoring rod twist together and rush downstream, catching the treadway. On the downstream side of the bridge, Bishop reaches into the water and fishes around until he snags the entangled lines. We slip and slide into position on the slippery pontoons and begin to heave. But the line is snagged on the bottom. Epps has already been underwater half a minute.

We jerk, the line breaks free, and we heave. Epps finally pops up a dozen feet downstream, puffing and spewing ice water. We work the line over to the shore and pull him to safety, blue with the cold, teeth clacking. Lafonte begins to untie the rope from his wrist, then stops and raises Epps' hand so that we can all see the line to the steel rod wrapped three or four times around Epps' wrist.

Bishop and Talley help Epps up the bank. Lafonte picks up the rod. "Let me see if I have this right," he says. "You put on a life-jacket and a life-line. Then you tie your arm to a hundred-pound rod and swan-dive into the Han. Is that right?"

"That's the Epps way."

We ate C-rations standing on the bank in shifts and worked without break until we had a bridge across the Han. Somebody christened it the Al Jolson Bridge. A lieutenant from battalion headquarters launched her maiden crossing in his jeep. He was halfway across when he was shot and killed.

The river began to rise with the tide. We weren't that far upriver from the harbor at Inchon, which has the largest tides in the world. We worked the rest of the day and all night with the Bridge Platoon installing transoms and cables so that the bridge could be raised and lowered. Third Division artillery had pounded the Chinese positions into silence, and the infantry had secured a large perimeter, so we didn't face any more incoming fire.

Early on March 18th, the Corps Engineers assumed control of the bridge, and we moved north to support the 64th Heavy Tank Battalion. Small, terraced hills stretched ahead of us to the foothills of the central mountain range, where we could see bombs and artillery exploding. Behind them, the high peaks seemed to gaze serenely...snow-covered and remote, unattached and uninterested in this passing spectacle. From the hilltops, we could see the roads clogged with fleeing peasants, up the gradual ascent of the Chorwon valley toward Uijongbu, which was being levelled. We began to pass burned-out trucks and tanks of the retreating Chinese forces.

We stopped early, in a wooded area a few miles south of Uijongbu, and immediately had a hot meal, courtesy of High Pockets Wilkinson and Bob Henley. They had modified the mess truck so that the cooks could work in transit. The tarp was raised for headroom and the cooking equipment was welded into place. There was a water line from the tank which was towed behind the truck. A converted Chinese motor pumped water into a sink similarly welded into place. On both sides, the canopies were adjustable over fold-up runways put together from bridge parts. No matter rain, snow or shine, the Mongrels could pull off the road, have a hot meal, and be back underway in an hour.

After chow, High Pockets and Bob Henley removed the tank and made a water run to Yongdungpo. When they returned, there was bubbly beer running over the top of the water truck. Pretty soon, there were long lines of Mongrels on both sides of the tank, canteen cups in hand. High Pockets brought a foamy five gallon water can into first squad's tent.

"If I get busted for this, I'm going to kill you," I said.

"Just relax, Kestner. We brought plenty of water, too. The cook told me that the Captain is staying in his tent. It's equipment maintenance and personal hygiene day tomorrow."

By now, the line around the water tank included tankers from the 64th Heavy Tankers and infantrymen from the 65th Infantry, waiting with five gallon water cans. A poker game started up in one end of the tent.

High Pockets set the water can at that end of the tent and filled his canteen cup. "You should try it," he said. "We sampled all the vats. This was the best."

"You guys are going to have to keep it down or you'll be outside digging foxholes."

Outside, an impromptu chorus was singing another chorus of Nat King Cole's "Mona Lisa." Every chorus featured a new sexual position. Some of them would have strained a contortionist.

"We'll be ok," Bishop said, "unless Talley starts his war dance." Talley hoisted his frothy canteen cup. "No war dances tonight."

Next morning, I had the the mess tent almost to myself. The cook told me that High Pockets had traded beer for fresh food, so we had fresh eggs and bacon. He also made biscuits and white gravy.

After chow, I walked back through the quiet camp to first squad tent, where the guys were sleeping it off, sprawled across their cots like compost, jerking and snorting in irregular raspy breaths. Except for their various grunts and snorts, the morning was so still that I could hear a drunken fly buzzing around the five gallon can with the beer.

I cleaned out old D-21, checked her oil and water, then drove her around for a fill up. I took inventory of the tools and then settled down for a long nap. I woke in time for lunch and sat with Talley, who decided to have a little lunch with his beer.

"You must have woke up with that beer in your hand," I said.

"It's an Indian trick," he said.

The Captain didn't come out of his tent the whole day. In the afternoon, High Pockets drove the tank back to the water point, and returned with water. He insisted the tanks had been cleaned first, but the water was rank for the next few days.

Next morning, the Captain called a company formation. He hoped we had taken advantage of the day off. We should enjoy today, he said, because tomorrow morning we were to move north with the 64th Heavy Tank Battalion. By the way, it was unconfirmed, but there were reports that Korean civilian workers had found the bodies of several dead Chinese soldiers in the beer vats at Yongdungpo.

That news didn't bother me, but there were sick Dogs around camp that day.

Chapter 6:

THE CRUELEST MONTH

General Ridgway had assumed command in dead winter, with Seoul skidding toward its third fall within the first six months of the war. His plans to launch an immediate offensive were delayed by the Communist advance, but even in that withdrawal, he insisted on continued close contact with enemy forces and an aggressive overall strategy of "maximum delay and maximum punishment."

When the combined North Korean and Chinese advance was contained, the subsequent offensives north to capture Seoul, for the fourth and final time of the war, were conducted under the code names Operation Killer and Operation Ripper. In March, 1951, Secretary of State Dean Rusk was requested to change those names. A member of the State Department wrote to him, saying, "I fear that to many people, Korea now means only killing, a process of killing Americans, Chinese, and Koreans."

Ridgway later wrote that he was "by nature, opposed to any effort to 'sell' war to people as an only mildly unpleasant business that requires very little in the way of blood." But he went along with it; the re-taking of Seoul was conducted under the new name, Operation Courageous. The advances north of the Han were called Operation Tomahawk and Operation Rugged, among others. Ironically, in spite of their toned-down euphemisms, they were among the bloodiest battles of the war.

The defensive/offensive pattern established by circumstance during the first months of '51 became deliberate strategy. Repeatedly, Eighth Army would advance against enemy positions and hold while enemy resistance increased. Precise artillery coordinates would be mapped out behind the line, mine-fields and booby-traps installed, and a withdrawal-to-entrap would be coordinated with close air support. Enemy forces would be lured into the trap and killed with calculated technological efficiency. UN superiority in firepower thus compensated for Communist superiority in manpower.

Uijongbu fell on the second morning of Operation Tomahawk, under a combined assault by the 15th Infantry Regiment from the southeast and the 64th Tankers and the 65th Infantry advancing from the southwest, along the Seoul road, where the Mongrels earlier had their beer festival. Air support included Air Force F-80's and Navy P-41's. Following that combined assault, Kulbes' Mongrels entered a city that had been reduced to a smokestack and a few still-standing walls surrounded by miles of concrete rubble. Broken, twisted plumbing pipes protruded into the air where walls had once been.

We bulldozed the road free of rubble and camped outside of town. Next morning, March 24, first squad was assigned to mine-clearing ahead of Company C of the 64th Heavy Tank Battalion. It was one of those spring days when the sunshine seems time-warped out of the middle of July to stir up the slow blood of winter. The road north rose ahead of us in long vistas of rolling, earthy hills, foreshortened and magnified by the sawtooth ridges rising behind them, blue and canyon-scarred.

We followed the road down the long back-slope of a hill to a wash where a bridge had been blown. John Grover and I left our field jackets in the truck and checked for mines on both sides of the bridge. To be safe, I walked under the bridge to check, and John met me there.

"Nothing," he said.

"Me, either," I said. "It's clear."

We started back to the road to signal an all clear to the tankers. John walked out the way I had come in, and, for no good reason, I went out the other way, so that our paths made an X.

John's body writhed in a burst of machine-gun fire for a second and fell onto the ground. I pulled him into shelter beneath the bridge while, overhead, tank cannons fired and the machine gun emplacement erupted in fragments. "Love," John said.

"Go easy," I said. I held my hand under his neck.

"Mother." He tried to sit up. "Tell her."

Sergeant Morton tried to convince me, later, that it didn't matter which side of the bridge John was on, but I would feel for a long time that he had taken fire intended for me.

The splendid day dragged by. I replayed that moment under the bridge over and over, wondering why we changed sides. There was no reason.

We finally returned to Uijongbu, and High Pockets decided to class up the joint. While most of the company was at chow, he fired up the bulldozer to clear a large concrete pad for the tents. An oxygen tank concealed beneath the rubble ruptured and jetted across the pad in jumpy, unpredictable bursts. Stones and masonry fragments pinged and snapped against the parked vehicles while the men of Dog Company ran this way and that looking for shelter. Finally the canister smashed into the side of a troop truck and whooshed still.

The battalion Chaplain led a memorial next morning and Captain Kulbes offered a brief eulogy for Pfc. John Grover, who was our first fatality since the Chosin. I had never lost a man under my command before, and since it was an equipment maintenance and personal hygiene day, I had more time than I wanted to wonder what would have happened if we hadn't changed sides under the bridge.

Rain slapping against the tent woke me in the middle of the night. It wasn't your gentle spring flowers rain, either, but hammer drops that beat the countryside into submission, roaring on the tent tarps, then, increasing in tempo and running under the edge of the tent and across the concrete pad. I rolled over in my cot and felt the depth of water with my hand. Two inches, puny to anyone who grew up next door to the Mississippi. I went back to sleep.

The next morning began with another memorial and eulogy. Pvt. Sammie Clifton had been wounded during the same tank patrol that claimed John Grover. He died during the stormy night. Following the service, the Captain told us that we would have another rest day and then we would work in support of a major offensive toward the Iron Triangle. It was an important staging area for the North Korean and Chinese forces and we would meet the enemy.

After company formation, I introduced two replacements to the rest of the guys in first squad: Corporal Ramon Cruz, out of a Puerto Rico unit, and Private David Jordan, out of a formerly all-black unit. They came to us as part of Third Division's policy of desegregation, and their addition made us, for the first time in Korea, All-Americans: Leland Lipscomb from California; High Pockets Wilkinson from Mississippi; Peter Talley was a Native American from Arizona; "Old Man" Walter Meters, in his forties, was from Iowa; Harold Leighton, from Nebraska; Eugene Florek, from Chicago; Jack Bishop, from Mississippi; Private Lafonte came from the Bronx; and me, river rat Kestner, from Missouri. Of course, the sqaud leader was there too...wherever he was from and where he should have never left.

We pulled out next morning in the dark and joined up with the 64th Tankers a mile or so north of the bridge where John Grover had died. First squad joined tanker Sergeant Charlie William's C Company. The tankers had become familiar faces to us by now. We took positions on the tanks and rolled north through the infantry perimeter, eventually dismounting into what was new and unfriendly territory.

The 15th Infantry Regiment moved abreast over the steep slopes while first squad walked the twisting mountain roads ahead of the tanks, searching for mines. I assigned Jack Bishop and Eugene Florek to work with the new guys, and the morning passed routinely. At lunch time, we took turns riding the tanks and eating C-Rations.

In the early afternoon, we came to the first high ridge where a steep road led down the other side and disappeared in a sharp downhill turn behind a bluff. It was a good spot for an ambush, and Sergeant Williams wisely called a halt at the ridge until the infantry could advance.

Peter Talley and I walked down the road into the valley looking for mines. Finding none, we returned to the ridge, where the tankers had thrown open their hatches for smoke breaks. Talley continued to the rear tanks of the convoy, where most of first squad were standing around, gabbing. Charlie Williams asked if I'd found any mines, and I stopped to talk to him for a moment before walking back.

When I reached the third tank, bullets zinged off the turret and the tank commander dropped out of sight, closing and fastening the hatch. Chinese soldiers streamed over the boulders at the top of the ridge beside the road and began to slide down the hillside toward the lead tanks, each one, it seemed, carrying a satchel pack of explosives, and firing directly at me. Every tank in the convoy had slammed tight its hatch. I climbed onto the tank beside me and hammered with my fists to be let inside. No luck. They had left me to die...the cowards.

The .50 caliber machine gun was sitting there idle, the enemy was there, and I was there, with my old grudge. I slung the M-1 over my shoulder and began to return fire. I quickly ran through to the end of the first belt of ammo. I reached back for another belt and joined it to the belt which was disappearing into the firing chamber, almost without missing a shot.

The turrets of the first three tanks swiveled, and each opened fire with their dual .30 caliber machine guns, but they were not in good positions for the work. My .50 caliber barrel began to turn blue and to smoke. Each fifth round is a tracer, and I could see that they were beggining to wobble. The rifling inside the barrel was burning out. I began to fire in short bursts, in a death-dealing routine. I would reach behind for the next belt while continuing to fire with one hand, raise the belt above my head and lay it on the turret, and hook the belts together.

I was working on the last of seven boxes of 105 rounds each when the remaining soldiers retreated back behind the ridge. There were spent casings all over the road beside the tank, hundreds of soldiers dead and dying on the hillside, and a throbbing roar in my ears.

I was wired with adrenalin and out of my mind. I wanted to drag the tankers onto the road and kick in their faces. I wanted General MacArthur at their courts-martial. I unscrewed the fuse from a grenade and dropped it inside the tank as soon as the hatch was opened.

"There go a bunch of cowards," I yelled, while they climbed from the hatch, leaped from the turret, and ran. When he realized that the grenade inside the tank was a dud the sergeant turned back, ready to square off.

I called him every low, despicable name I knew, with my face about two inches from his. He reached for my collar. I pushed his hand away. The infantry arrived and separated us. Sergeant Williams pulled the commander around to the front of the tank.

"You've ruined my .50 caliber," the tanker yelled.

"You're lucky you're alive," I yelled back.

"Kestner!" Sergeant Williams yelled. "We're moving out. Get your squad together." I rounded the guys up and we took covering positions along the ridge.

What happened wasn't pretty. The infantry had already advanced past the ridge so that the enemy regiment was trapped between their rifle fire and the the tanks advancing toward them, .30 caliber machine guns blazing. They were shot and run down and mashed like melons beneath the tank tracks, but they refused to surrender until most of them were dead.

Infantry MPs took charge of the prisoners and we continued north. In the late afternoon, we arrived at a wide river valley. Still riding the tanks, we moved across the valley, everybody watching the uphill road which curved out of sight. A Russian T-34 tank rounded the hill and sped down the road toward us. I was sitting on Charlie Williams' turret when all the tankers in the battalion fired their .90 mm. cannons in unison, belching dense smoke and fire. The Russian tank disintegrated.

As the tankers set up a defensive perimeter, I could only wonder if I would ever be able to hear again.

First squad moved north the next morning on an assignment to repair roads behind the 64th tankers, who made pig wallows out of the roads. At an entirely ordinary spot, we passed their hand-painted sign: "You are crossing the 38th Parallel. Courtesy of the 64th Heavy Tank Battalion."

For the next few days, we repaired roads in the spring rains, working our way north toward the Imjin River. The 15th Regiment and the 64th Tank along with several other attached units had already crossed. East of us, the 65th Infantry and the 937th Field Artillery Battalion were pounding the town of Chorwon. Third Division was at full-bore, open-throttle, doing what it does best: imparting desolation and ruin upon the enemy.

On April 11, General Soule's jeep sped past us, heading north. He didn't stop to ask me how I thought the war was going either. I learned what happened next through the Korean Network of War Intelligence & News Gathering (KNOWING); in other words, his driver told Captain Kulbes' driver who told High Pockets, who told everybody.

The rainy spring sped up snow melt in the mountains. The normal intensity of the run-off was aggravated by the effects of a year of war: bombed and burned-out hillsides quickly eroded, adding tons of topsoil and uprooted vegetation to the overflowing rivers. The cable supporting the main bridge across the Imjin River snapped, sending pontoons and treadways rolling downriver.

Chinese and North Korean forces immediately recognized that UN forces north of the Imjin could be trapped with no means of effective withdrawal. They relocated units and began a major assault. Elements of the 7th and 15th Regiments, along with the 64th Heavy Tank Battalion and an attached Belgian unit found themselves in sudden fatal jeopardy.

General Soule met Colonel Gross, commander of the Tenth Combat Engineer's Battalion, on the south bank of the Imjin. We tried to send a power boat across with a straw line," the Colonel said, "but it lost power and washed downstream."

"I've ordered a floating bridge.It'll be here today," said General Soule.

"I'll bring up two companies," the Colonel responded, "But it'll take a while."

"We dont have a while," General Soule snapped back, "I passed Kulbes and his Mongrels a few miles back. Get them up here. Those war dawgs will get the bridge across in a hurry."

Colonel Gross grabbed a radio from his jeep.

"Bull Dog Six! Bull Dog Six! This is Skybridge Six. Over."

"Skybridge Six!" the answer came. "This is Bull Dog Six. Over."

"Bull Dog Six. How soon can you relocate your company to the Imjin?" asked the Colonel.

"A. S. A. P!" came Captain Kulbes' reply. "We are leaving right now."

"Bull Dog Six. Roger that" Colonel Gross responded, "This is Skybridge Six! Out!

Fifteen minutes later, the first Mongrels were rolling north.

Chapter 7:

CROSSING THE SAME RIVER TWICE

The Chorwon valley is a wide river valley, ringed by volcanic peaks on three sides, and descending gradually to the west, where the Imjin joins the Han on the way to the Yellow Sea. At the site of the washed-out bridge, the river is almost level with its surrounding landscape, and the banks of the river are barren strips of current-washed sand and river rock. Jagged boulders jut from the rushing brown surface of the river.

Dog Company arrived, mid-morning, at a scene of barely-contained chaos. Artillery units fired at northern enemy positions almost without pause; pedestrians quick-timed to their destinations; supply trucks unloaded and ambulances waited to load. As we approached the frenetic perimeter, a southbound jeep passed us on the narrow muddy road at about fifty MPH, horn blaring.

North of the river, the road curved over and around the small saddleback of a knoll, which supported a few pine trees. Trucks and jeeps of the trapped Belgian Battalion lined both sides of the muddy road. In the rainy distance, artillery rounds exploded. Sporadically, there was answerering fire by Chinese artillery, the whistle of the shells approaching, and the crash of their explosion.

We tried unsuccessfully to fire a marlin line across the river with a rocket launcher, and then we were fresh out of ideas. The river was fast, snow-cold, and rocky, but it was only about a hundred yards across, not much of a river compared to the Mississippi. I told Sergeant Morton I could go upriver a quarter mile or so and swim across with a tow line.

Sergeant Morton said I was nuts. I said that wasn't the issue. He said I would hit a rock. I said I wouldn't. He said I would freeze before I got across. I said maybe.

We talked to Lieutenant Smith and then to Captain Kulbes. "What if you hit a rock?" the Captain asked.

"I'll swim around them, sir."

"Unless someone else can come up with something," he said, "it's the only idea we have."

I got the squad together and told them my plan.

"What if you hit a rock?" High Pockets asked.

"I'm not going to hit a rock."

"Oh," he said. "Good plan."

We positioned a man every hundred feet along the bank to feed out the tow lines—I'd decided to carry two with me.

About a quarter mile above the bridge site, I stripped to my drawers and a t-shirt, put on a helmet liner and life-jacket, pressed the helmet liner tight, strapped it closed, and tied the lines around my waist.

Jack Bishop said he'd tell my mother how I died.

"Wait till I'm dead first," I said, and waded in.

Instantly, the bones in my legs and feet ached with cold, and my skin grew numb. I sat suddenly into the water and pushed off with no time to think about it. The current ripped me downstream so fast that I couldn't hold my trajectory. I concentrated on placing one arm in front of another, my head underwater, coming up for air every four strokes. Midway, I scraped my stomach over a boulder that tumbled me over and over and pulled my drawers down below my knees. I inhaled icy water through my nose into my lungs and coughed. I reached down to pull off my drawers and lost my helmet liner. I was numb. My arms moved slower and slower.

Hands grabbed and pulled me upright. "You're a brave little chap," a Luxembourg officer said. "Don't look now, but I think you've lost your trousers."

"Sir, do you have the line?"

Someone led me up the bank.

"Get this chap into a truck so he doesn't freeze," the officer shouted.

"Do you have the line? Sir?"

"We have both the line."

"Are you sure?"

"We have it."

Medics led me to a squad truck, removed the life-jacket and t-shirt, lighted a lantern for heat, and began to rub my limbs. A Belgian Colonel peeked under the truck tarp. "Lad, that was a brave thing," he said.

"Well sir," I answered. "I've swum the Mississippi, so this wasn't that big a deal." He handed me some woolen fatigues that more or less fit.

The Belgians pulled a straw line across with the tow line, then used that to pull a cable across. First squad hooked onto the cable and ferried across in assault boats, where they found me drinking sweet hot tea and munching a sweet roll. Ahhhh...Army Life!

We began digging for bridge anchors and medics began to ferry the first of the wounded back across the river. By the time the bridging trucks arrived, at twilight, we had dug in and installed three cable anchors. Captain Kulbes wasn't going to watch a bridge built by D Company float down the river.

In darkness, we crossed back over to help inflate pontoons and install treadways, working and sleeping in two hour shifts. About ten the next morning, incoming artillery exploded beyond the bridging truck which was hoisting the treadways into place. There was brief silence while the artillery commanders in the rear area locked in the location of the enemy piece, then a volley of return fire.

Two engineers from the battalion bridge company had been killed by the incoming round: Corporal William Scalf, and Corporal Sonnie Holmes. On the opposite side of the 10-ton truck, two Mongrels escaped with shrapnel wounds.

By mid-day, the first ambulances loaded with wounded crossed from the north bank, and Third Corps Engineers assumed maintenance of the bridge. General Soule congratulated the Captain, and the war dawgs headed south, to hot chow and dry sleep.

The long-range forecast was for rain and swollen rivers and muddy, torn-up roads. We repaired the same roads again and again, dressed in ponchoes, up to our boot-tops in mire, never completely dry. A tank battalion or supply convoy would pass through, and we would start over.

It was a welcome change of pace when we were assigned to rebuild a Bailey Bridge across the Hantan River near the town of Kumhwa. Along with Chorwon and Pyonggang, Kumhwa forms the reference points of the Iron Triangle. The bridge abutments were sound. We hooked onto the wrecked metal spans with the company dozer, pulled them into the river, and installed the new Bailey in three hours.

Back at Uijongbu, we read in Stars and Stripes that Truman had fired MacArthur. MacArthur's reputation for saving lives made him a soldier's general. Truman, on the other hand, mistrusted the military, but the feeling was mutual. He had dangerously downsized in the late forties, and he refused to provide adequate forces or support for the war in Korea. He had created what was called the Truman Year, which doubled the amount of time soldiers were exposed to the jeopardy of combat. Worse, for me, Truman and I were both from Missouri. During the next week, until Captain Kulbes put a stop to it, Truman was the subject of endless belly-aching.

Bed Check Charlie became a regular visitor. We'd just get settled in, dry, fed, ready to dream. Out of the north would come the drone of the propeller, the camp alarm would sound, everybody would wake up and run to the foxholes and watch the plane buzz past. I traded with an artillery unit for an anti-aircraft ground, mounted for a .50 caliber machine gun, scrounged 6 cases of ammunition and set up an anti-aircraft post behind camp.

The plane would approach and the alarm would sound. I would strap on my boots and run to the outpost, sometimes dressed only in my trousers, listen for the drone of the engine in the black sky, and fire. One night, Bed Check Charlie dropped what I think was a 120mm mortar shell into the Dog's camp, and tore up the field kitchen.

We ate C-Rations until the kitchen could be re-supplied. It was clear to everybody that Gung-Ho Kestner was responsible for drawing the fire which destroyed our kitchen and it didn't help my reputation any that Truman and I were both from Missouri. But I didn't stop trying to take out Bed Check Charlie.

I heard, through the Korean Network of Wartime Intelligence and News Gathering (KNOWING), which is to say, the Captain's driver told High Pockets, who then told everybody else, that Captain Kulbes was getting grief from battalion about the attitude of the Mongrels:

Colonel Gross: Captain, your men are too damned cocky.

Captain Kulbes: They have esprit de corps. Sometimes that's all they have going for them.

Colonel Gross: The other companies behave better. Maybe you set a bad example.

Captain Kulbes: They drive themselves. If I asked them to build a road through a mountain, they would do it just to prove they could. Are you suggesting that I stifle that?

Colonel Gross: I'm not suggesting anything, but they're too damned cocky.

Captain Kulbes: I don't want to lower their morale.

Colonel Gross: What the hell ever.

It was true. We did anything the Captain asked. And a few things he didn't. First squad was notorious for its thievery. Most of the credit for this goes to High Pockets. There was always a junk yard collection of motors and armaments somewhere around the squad tent that he and Bishop had liberated on some excursion or other.

Old D-21, or more properly, Gloria, purred. She always had new engine parts and headlights, windshield wipers, tarps and sideboards. Bishop and High Pockets would time their visits to the transportation pool when the motor squad was at a movie or something. They'd find a new truck and savage it, leaving Gloria's old equipment in exchange.

The motor sergeant who had wanted to scrap her back at Pusan hadn't worked on her a minute. He was suspicious of her condition, often asking if it were time for maintenance and a check-up.

"Thanks anyway, Sarge. High-Pockets keeps her in good shape." I knew that if he ever got his greasy fingernails on her, he would scrap her out.

"She does look in good shape," he would say. "Where did you find all those new parts?"

"Here and there, Sarge. We trade for them. You know."

One day, High Pockets got a Dear John letter from his girlfriend and painted four coats of paint over her name on the hood. A week later he was made platoon equipment operator. Jack Bishop was made the new driver, so he quickly painted his girlfriend's name, Amy, on the hood.

The Captain decided he had heard enough about Truman. At Company Formation, he explained that the Army was not a democracy. Soldiers sacrificed many of their civil rights. To threaten the President or the Congress was a treasonable offense. If somebody had a complaint about the way the war was handled, that person should talk to him, personally. Otherwise, there would be a court-martial. There would be no more whining and belly-aching in Dog Company.

In late April, the Communist forces began what would be their last major offensive toward Seoul. As part of the withdrawal of Third Division toward the Han, we were reassigned to the Iron Triangle to destroy the Bailey Bridge..the same bridge we had installed a mere two weeks before. We set up camp late inside a perimeter established by the 15th Infantry and the 64th Heavy Tankers. Next morning, while we mined the bridge, we began to receive sniper fire from the ridges above us.

We destroyed the bridge just ahead of an assault by enemy infantry and retreated to camp, but the secure perimeter previously held by the tankers and the infantry had vanished. We joined headquarters platoon in removing what we could, then burned our tents and blew the explosives we didn't have time to take with us. About a mile south we pulled in behind the line held by the withdrawing infantry and tankers. Air support covered our withdrawal to Yon Chon.

We set up camp well behind the field artillery, just outside the village, ate C-Rations standing up, and squeezed in a ragged sleep in pup tents. In first light next morning, a spotter in the village mistook our pole trailers for howitzers. Rounds whistled in and exploded, sending wood and metal splinters flying.

Lieutenant Smith and his driver, Glenn Taylor, were walking to the Lieutenant's jeep when they heard the unmistakeable screech of incoming artillery and leaped for cover in a ditch, beside High Pockets. They stayed down until the barrage was clearly past, then picked themselves out of the dirt to find that the jeep trailer had been hit, destroying the trunk with Lieutenant Smith's things. He walked around the trailer, trying to save what he could.

He handed a jagged corner of shaped felt to High-Pockets. "My campaign hat from Merrill's Marauders," he said.

"That's a bad deal, sir," High Pockets responded.

"Sir...?" said Glenn Taylor.

Lieutenant Smith rummaged through the smashed debris looking for his smoking pipes and found only meershaum and briar fragments.

"They got all my pipes, too," he said.

"Yes, sir," High Pockets commisserated.

Lieutenant Smith looked for his custom tobacco, shipped half-way around the globe. "And all my tobacco," he said.

"It's a bad deal, sir," High Pockets answered.

"Look at my transom," Lieutenant Smith said, holding up a broken eye-glass still housed in a jagged, partial cylinder. High Pockets gathered paper fragments from the ground and repeated, "It's a bad deal, all right, sir."

"Sir...?" Glenn Taylor repeated.

"Oh, never mind, Corporal," Lieutenant Smith answered. "No one was injured." He looked up from the broken eye-glass of his transom and noticed for the first time that Glenn Taylor had been slightly wounded and was waiting patiently, bleeding. Then he niticed himself that he too was bleeding. He had been hit!

"Damn!" Lieutenant Smith yelled, and walked with Taylor to the supply tent where the medics were stationed. Taylor was treated and bandaged and back on duty a half hour later.

We packed up our tents, hurrying to stay ahead of the advancing enemy. We heated C-Rations in an immersion heater in the mess tent and ate outside where we could drop everything and run if necessary. A new man, only two days in Korea, Pfc. Steve Zagurskie, who was washing his mess kit, died when an artillery round screeched in and exploded in the wash can.

We moved south, stabilizing roads ahead of the Third Division troops, who were withdrawing into successive defensive positions. From line Wyoming, they withdrew to the Kansas line, north of the Hantan. From there, they established three successive no-name lines until they were only a few miles north of Seoul. Hordes of enemy died in ill-advised pursuit down mined roads, across terrain carefully mapped and coordinated for artillery fire, beneath napalm bombs. The carnage stunk. A soldier told a reporter from Time magazine, "they're spending people the way we spend ammunition."

When we reached the Han, we spent several nights in the same camp, continuing daily repairs on the road to Uijonbgu. The Communist plan to retake Seoul by May Day slowly dissolved in the face of I Corps' continuing punishment, and they began to withdraw north of Uijongbu to regroup. It had been the largest single battle of the Korean War, with 70,000 Communist and 7,000 UN casualties. The 3rd Infantry Division was in the forward area of Seoul and took the brunt of the CCF's offensive to retake Seoul. However, General Soule's 3d would stop them cold in their tracks!

On our second night north of the Han, Bed Check Charlie found us and dropped a mortar round on our new mess tent.

Chapter 8:

EAST OF WONJU

We crossed the Han and drove through the rubble of Seoul to the matching rubble of its sister city, Yongdungpo, where we would spend the first two weeks of May behind the lines. We were assigned a ghost looey who was punching in the slot on his resume under the category of "combat experience." A dedicated tent hog, he spent so much time inside that nobody was sure what he did, if anything, or when he left, if he did leave. For all I know, he may still be wandering the streets of Yongdungpo, looking for the headquarters tent, with a folder of Morning Reports under his arm and a pencil balanced above his ear, saying, "Let's see. Where was I?"

We maintained roads and repaired bridges along the Han in workaday routine. Passing soldiers would occasionally shoot the bridge pontoons, out of boredom, or for practice, or just to prove that they might be in Korea but they damn well felt no sense of obligation about it. The perimeter was secure, and we kept a minimal night-time patrol. The mess tent was replaced, and because we were stationed in the rich side pocket of I Corps, the cooks had fresh provisions: steaks, home-made spaghetti, chili, and hamburgers for dinner, orange juice, fresh eggs and bacon for breakfast. If you judged by the menu, we might have been in Kansas City.

Behind the lines is a little bit lazy, even boring, for an eighteen year old immortal. I spent the evenings reading FM-5-34, the Combat Engineer's Manual, or hanging out with Sergeant Morton in the 2nd Platoon tent, but some of the guys found time for more gripping pastimes.

On the outskirts of town there had begun to appear all the camp-followers whose object was soldier's pay. This included women and children who asked to do laundry or shine shoes for a few coins. It also included crippled beggars and overnight "clubs" that offered liquor, gambling, music and sex. A lot of stripes were lost in front of the Captain the morning after. Here would come the MPs with a couple of hung-over, red-eyed, dissheveled Mongrels, there would go their stripes, and for the next week, or weeks, there they would be, peeling them spuds, policing them latrines.

The MPs showed up one morning with a particularly ripe project. When the MPs caught him, at some off-limits dive with a juke box and friendly hostesses on the edge of town, Epps had run for it, through a back exit, along a berm, across a rice paddy, and chest-deep into a newly-thawed and extravagantly fragrant honey hole. The MPs caught him, drunk and incoherent, wrapped him in a poncho, and stuffed him into an artillery ammo box they pushed as far into the back of the jeep as they could.

After they dumped him at Dog Company, the headquarters sergeant and his squad had him remove his clothes and doused him repeatedly with buckets of cold water until he was more or less clean. But there was method in Epps' madness, I suspect. Every day that he was on KP was a day he missed work details and combat assignments.

I'd already had more than enough of Yongdungpo when we received a sudden assignment to move ASAP halfway across Korea, to Wonju, a shattered village high in the center of the peninsula. The North Korean Peoples' Army and the Consolidated Chinese Army had mounted an offensive down the central mountains. If they could take Wonju, they might drive west and encircle Seoul.

We were on the road in under an hour. We caravaned south to Suwon, then west to Yoju, across the Han one more time, which was a much smaller river here, near its source, than it was at Seoul. From Yoju, we drove up the valley to Wonju, following the signs left for us by Lieutenant Taggart, a first rate officer out of West Point in charge of Lieutenant Rosen's former third platoon.

Wonju had been flattened by almost as many successive conquests and reconquests as Seoul. We arrived in the late afternoon and were directed by MPs onto a narrow road bulldozed through rubble, northeast. We stopped in a canyon where twin railroad tunnels had been blasted though the mountain, though we still hadn't made contact with either the 15th Infantry Regiment or the 64th Heavy Tankers.

Captain Kulbes, who seemed worried, called a formation and laid out for us his plans for a solid defensive perimeter. We set up a road block with tank traps so that the infantry, presumedly north of us, could withdraw into our interior, if necessary. We set up a line of machine gun emplacements from one hill-top to another overlooking the road entering the canyon from the north, each one connected to headquarters with a direct phone hook-up. The line itself was an infantry defense, a three man unit every thirty feet, dug into foxholes and overarmed with ammunition, grenades, and rocket-launchers. We set rigging charges in the road. Behind that first line, we strung concertina from one hillside, through the river, to the other hillside, and positioned soldiers with rocket launchers on both banks.

Talley and I manned a machine-gun placement on a hillside that would give a squirrel vertigo. North of us, we could hear vehicles moving. Captain Kulbes called frequently throughout the night.

"Kestner, what can you see?"

"Nothing, sir. Talley and I can hear troop movements, though."

"Can you estimate the distance?"

"Five, six miles. They seem to be coming this way. We should be able to see at daybreak."

I could hear that he was worried, and that made me worried. The vehicles north of us would stop, and we would guess they had camped for the night. Then we would hear them again, closer. At daybreak, a runner came up with C-Rations. The troop movements sounded about a mile away, but we still hadn't been able to see anything.

A jeep bounced up the road from Wonju, and Captain Kulbes saluted the infantry Colonel who sat in the passenger seat. Troop trucks arrived behind the jeep, and the 15th infantry began to dismount.

The Colonel stepped down from his jeep. "Captain Kulbes, did you realize that there are at least two enemy regiments headed this way?"

"That's about normal for the Mongrels," the Captain said.

"We thought you were coming from Yongdungpo. How did you get here so fast?"

"We had orders to move ASAP, Colonel."

The Colonel asked him to hold and maintain the defensive perimeter while the infantry advanced. The soldiers, who were already forming up, moved quickly and silently into the hills. A squad passed near Talley and me, steady and lethal, on their way to work. I like the infantry. Everything is vulnerable to it.

Far behind us, Division Long-Toms began to thunder, F-80's and B-25s passed overhead, and the mountain north of us began to shake and burn. The unmistakeable odor of napalm drifted across the valley, and we heard the first infantry fire, less than a mile away. Talk about lucky. If the infantry had arrived twenty minutes later, those two pitful enemy regiments would have had to face the humiliation of getting their butts kicked by Kulbes' Mongrels.

We held our positions until mid-afternoon, when the outcome of the battle in front of us was no longer in question. Captain Kulbes received orders to pull back, and we arrived in twilight at Wonju, where C Company of the 64th Heavy Tank Battalion and the 9th field artillery battery had been held in reserve.

Before we had even settled in, a South Korean officer came out of the mountains. He explained that the enemy forces had splintered and at least a full regiment, with attached units, about 3,000 soldiers, was advancing on our positions.

Captain Kulbes was selected by the other unit officers as Task Force Commander, and we set up a defensive line facing north across a large open field. There were fifteen M-46 tanks, each with a .90 mm cannon, two .30 caliber and one .50 caliber machine guns. Behind that armored line was the battery of .105mm Howitzers of the 9th Field Artillery Battalion. The Mongrels dug into foxholes in covering support of the armor and artillery and positioned our four .50 caliber machine guns so that intersecting fire covered the whole field.

The squad leader served as liaison to the command post as long as he could, but finally joined Fisher and Cruz in their shallow fox-hole. There hadn't been enough time to get really dug in.

Sergeant Morton walked the line. "Kestner! Do you hear anything?"

"Nothing, Sarge."

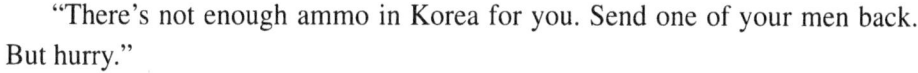
Franklin Kestner, 1st Squad Leader; with Thunder Pass in the background.

"Who's there with you?"

"Talley and LaFonte."

"You guys need anything?"

"More ammo."

"There's not enough ammo in Korea for you. Send one of your men back. But hurry."

I tapped Talley, who scrambled away.

"Bring me a beer and a pastrami sandwich," LaFonte yelled.

Tom Ortega, who was manning the .50 caliber in the next emplacement, yelled to Talley that he would like to order tacos and beer.

I ate my brown cake and the wind bounced my discarded C-Ration container around behind a tank. I opened my chiclets. Talley returned with two boxes of .50 caliber ammunition.

I hadn't heard a single whine from first squad since we'd left Yongdungpo...they might turn out to be warriors after all. Facing a regiment of Chinese soldiers on a dark night could break them, though. Chinese tactics were frustrating and unnerving: uncoordinated, wavering bugles blowing here and there, raspy noise-makers like a New Year's party in Times Square, irregular bass drums beating, then, maybe, nothing. Then, more noise-makers, signalling who knew what?

There came a single rifle shot from somewhere east of us, in the third platoon's section of the line, and the dual headlights on all fifteen tanks instantly flared on, freezing an advancing line of Chinese soldiers, wrapped in almost indistinguishable gray against the line of trees where they were emerging. In the instant of time it takes for a flash-bulb to pop, we stared at them, trapped like deer in headlights. Then, murderous hell.

There came the racking of nearly fifty machine guns, the crash of cannons and artillery, bugles, bass drums, rifle fire, smoke, the stench of cordite, the cries of the wounded, somebody nearby calling for a flashlight, Talley telling me to move my leg so he could insert the next belt of ammunition, the ping of rifle fire deflected off the tanks, the POP of an exploding headlight, the turret on the tank behind us spinning to aim, the crash again of its .90 mm cannon with the smoke and dust swirling around the foxhole, and the explosion of howitzer rounds landing...screams following all.

The first wave ended as unpredictably as it had begun. The tank lights snapped off. "I wish we had more ammo," Talley said.

There were moans and sobs, screeches, groans, from the wounded in the field ahead of us. Behind us, Morton yelled to ask how we were doing. "No casualties," I said.

Bugles wavered, the noise-makers rattled, then were silent. "Weird," LaFonte said. Behind us, the howitzers whirred as the barrels were lowered almost level.

The second assault meant business.

A first shot sounded, and tank headlights flared on. The enemy ran toward us in a suicidal frontal assault. Howitzer rounds and tank cannon fire sizzled overhead and detonated among the bodies, and a scythe-like blanket of machine-gun fire cut down wave after wave. Here and there, a lone, brave, desperate, pitiful soldier would advance out of the ranks of his downed comrades to maybe twenty yards from the line before being killed by rifle fire.

I'd forgotten the nausea, but it flooded back when the second wave withdrew, and the mineral, hot smell of blood mixed with the rank stench of cordite. Their whole offensive depended on taking Wonju, and with their other regiment decimated by the 15th Infantry, I suppose their commanders didn't feel they could withdraw, no matter the cost.

They sacrificed themselves on the altar of who knows what god. Wave after wave, their fallen comrades like so many hurdles to leap on their way to the rough embrace of the beast. A long lull in the early morning was followed by another major assault. Again, just before dawn, they launched a weak assault on First Platoon that was quickly and thouroughly repulsed. Then, we waited.

As dawn approached, the runners came with coffee. Morton passed behind the line. "Are you guys ok?"

"Fine, Sarge."

"We may not have taken a single casualty," he said.

Two battalions of the Seventh Infantry arrived to rescue us. They moved out in a hurry after the fleeing remnants of enemy, while Medics roamed the field searching for survivors. "You guys did really good," I said to the squad.

We'd been at it two days and nights, but we could sleep most of the day. At dinner, High Pockets told us that we had withstood a regimental assault without taking a single casualty, and the Infantry Colonel was proposing Captain Kulbes for a Congressional Medal of Honor. The Colonel was also proposing a Presidential Unit Citation for all the involved units.

The Colonel had arrived in the silence after the battle and found men walking here and there, drinking coffee and chatting, and it wasn't until he saw the bodies in the field that he understood what had happened.

"Everything happened." LaFonte said. "All at once."

"There were hordes of those guys," Bishop said.

"How many men are there in a horde?" Talley asked.

"Go count 'em," LaFonte said.

At company formation after dinner, Captain Kulbes confirmed, from the front bumper of his jeep, that we were being written up for a Presidential Unit Citation. Best of all, he said, no casualties had been taken. Not one. He congratulated us for a job well done and said we would move back north in the morning. He wished us good dreams. He said nothing about his own nomination for the Medal of Honor.

Starry night, and calm: I turned in early, slept a single long dream and woke before the First Sergeant's whistle. I lay there, hands behind my head, the tent roof flapping in the quiet morning, breakfast coming right up, a long drive ahead of us and no worries for the day. A breeze passed through the mesh window over my cot, caressing me. Let's see...how did that dream go? Somebody in the tent belched and turned in his cot. Ah, the Army!

But it was still a dream driving north, watching the landscape where we had fought vanish behind us. Then, across the Han for the fifth or sixth time. At Suwon, we pulled off the road for lunch. Back onto the road, we crossed the Han the second time that day, across the Al Jolson bridge we had helped build, then northeast toward Uijongbu and the Iron Triangle, the shadows of the mountains beginning to lie down long across the valleys.

This Korea was a farmer's dream, with its deep, mineral-rich soil and ample water, and it was planting time. My body recognized it before my mind did. I supposed my father would have his acres plowed and ready for planting. In twilight, we set camp in a spot where we had camped before. We ate the last steaks we would have for a while, with french fries and ketchup, whole sweet corn, cook's white bread, pudding and coffee. I turned in early and thought about my dad, about how pretty Korea could be, about how first squad was toughening up, about anything except what had happened east of Wonju.

Chapter 9:

COMBAT STRIPES

Although they would launch other attacks, their failed May offensives were the last time Chinese and North Korean forces would ever remotely threaten Seoul. Increasingly, the war would be fought a few miles north or south of the 38th Parallel. We would advance north and hold until they launched a counter-offensive, then initiate one more strategic withdrawal-to-entrap. They would advance into hell-fire, dying by thousands against our pre-planned and precisely coordinated air and artillery barrages.

The drive north was conducted under the code name Pile Driver. We went through Uijongbu, northeast nearly to Kumhwa, where our artillery fired endlessly against a dug-in enemy. We rebuilt the Bailey Bridge across the Hantan, southwest of Kumhwa, that we had already rebuilt once and destroyed once. We strung barbed wire and planted mines in preparation for the Chinese counter-offensives that were sure to come. We widened and filled roads and reinforced damaged bridges and culverts on the Uijongbu to Kumhwa main supply route, falling into a work-a-day routine as predictable as in a state-side construction company.

Here and there around the Chorwon valley, refugee families began to return to their homes for spring planting. Several times, our Medics provided treatment for farmers who stepped on mines in their rice paddies.

One morning a squad in third platoon built a fire over a buried mortar shell and the heat set the shell off. Their wounds weren't serious, but they asked for Purple Hearts. The platoon sergeant said thay had set the fire themselves. Yeah, but it was an enemy shell, they argued. I figured that debate would have lasted about ten seconds if Lieutenant Rosen had still been in charge.

At the end of May, we relocated to a semi-permanent camp south of the bridge across the Imjin River. We began to receive Korean civilians laborers, as many as 250 a day, to build more permanent roads, with culverts and bridges in low areas susceptible to run-off, and to work in shifts around the clock.

Regular, drizzly spring rains meant we worked in mud, slogged through mud, ate and slept in mud. Bishop got a Dear John letter from his girlfriend and painted over her name on the hood. D-21 was jealous.

One morning in early June, Sergeant Morton and Lieutenant Smith showed up in the lieutenant's jeep while first squad was putting away tools at the end of a long night shift. "Tell your squad leader to get the men home and hop in the jeep with us," Morton said. I slugged over to the cab of D-21 to tell the Corporal, returned, kicked off as much mud as I could on the front tire of the jeep, and took a seat in the back.

The lieutenant backed up the jeep and turned around.

"Hey, Kestner! What do you think about the kind of job you've been doing?" Morton asked.

"I've been trying," I said. "Have I done something wrong?"

Lieutenant Smith passed a sheet of paper back to me. "Read this."

>Battalion Special Order.
>Kestner, Franklin D. R., RA17279252,
>is promoted from Private, First Class
>to Corporal, E-4. By order of Colonel Gross.

"Thank you two for this," I said.

"You deserve to be Corporal," Lieutenant Smith said. "Besides, a squad leader needs that rank. Your present leader is transferring to the first platoon as a construction specialist, and you're taking over tomorrow morning."

"I had the tool man find Corporal stripes and sew them on one of your shirts," Morton said. He turned in his seat. "Give me your helmet liner first."

I passed the helmet liner up.

He turned and hurled it twenty yards into a rice paddy.

"That's a good helmet liner, Sarge."

"But it doesn't have Corporal stripes," he said. "Here."

He passed me a liner with Corporal stripes. "And put this on, too." He passed me the shirt, with its combat stripes sewn in place. Combat stripes are thicker and heavier than service stripes. All that power and authority weighted down my arm when I put it on.

Back at camp, they congratulated me again. "You've been running the squad for a long time anyway," Lieutenant Smith said. "If anything, the promotion is overdue."

Morton and I went to chow. First squad showed up, and Morton told the squad leader (the former squad leader) that his transfer had come through. "Corporal Kestner will be taking over."

"Corporal Kestner?" he asked.

"Yep."

"But he's eighteen years old."

"Yep."

"Lord have mercy!" High Pockets said, after Morton had left. "He was already hard to live with. Now he won't let us stay in the same tent."

"High Pockets!" I commanded.

"Yes, Corporal?"

"You're talking to a field-grade, U.S. Army non-commissioned officer."

"Yes, Corporal."

Now that I could shape the squad with more iron, my old nickname, Little Caesar, became modified to Little Caesar and his Legion. First squad was assigned to screening patrol more often than the other squads, was first to receive daily assignments, and first in line for chow at the end of the day. We began to swagger. I pushed us to our limits, especially on patrols, trying to see how much ground we could cover, how many prisoners we could take. When the guys in third platoon finally got their Purple Hearts, we snickered and called them campfire casualties.

The enemy roamed behind the lines in guerilla units so that we had always to be alert for snipers. Larger enemy units often brought their mighty military prowess to bear against peasant villages, even those of their own countrymen north of the 38th Parallel. After Wonju, I'd begun to pity them for being led by leaders who demanded such deathly self-sacrifice against our more disciplined and better-equipped army. Their brutal willingness to exterminate whole families who only scratched out farmer's livings churned my stomach and kept my old grudge alive.

We moved on patrol in silent, effective coordination. Sgt. Davies, the new assistant squad leader, walked the second point, bringing up one line of the wedge. Often enough, we'd approach a village we'd passed through before and find it desolate, empty of people, voices, movement, the spring planting going to weeds. Once in a while we were lucky. A few hand signals, and Davies' section would be moving into position. Bishop would lead the second section into covering positions in the other direction. Talley and I would move forward, into firing range, and wait.

When the signal came back that the men were in position, I'd sight in the one enemy who was enjoying his last few breaths and challenge him with a round. Maybe the enemy would fire a few answering rounds, to test the perimeter, and be met with a volley of fire from a dozen encircling positions. Most often they shouted their familiar refrain, "GI Number One No Shoot!", threw their weapons to the ground and began bowing and scraping, glad to be out of it.

Word came that guerrillas had infiltrated a near-by camp and killed a whole squad asleep in their tents. In addition to a strengthened perimeter patrol, we began to keep someone on guard at all times inside the tent. He would be in charge of an alarm clock set to go off at five minutes past the hour. On the hour, he would wake the next man in rotation, who would set the alarm ahead, to five minutes past the next hour. The man on guard could sit in his cot as long as he was in his boots and his M-1 was ready. The system led to my first leadership failure. I woke one night, in darkness, and after a second realized the alarm had woke me. I waited another second, expecting the sound to end, and when it didn't, slipped into my boots, buckled up, and huffed down the center aisle in a growing rage to the cot of the offender. His legs were bent at the knees over one side of the cot, his feet still on the ground, and he was holding the alarm clock against his chest with one hand while the other arm hung over the side of the cot nearly to the floor, where his M-1 had fallen. His head had fallen straight back over the side of the cot from his feet and his sleeping breath fluttered in and out, on the verge of snoring.

    I was wide awake and jumpy with adrenalin. I turned his cot on its side spilling him to the floor and kicked him awake. "What kind of idiot are you?"

    He pushed the cot upright and stood, the alarm still sounding from the floor where it fell. He looked around the tent and rubbed his face with his hand. A few flashlights were turned on. I pushed him against the tent pole. "If you don't want to live, I'll take a pick handle to you." I twisted and pulled him by an arm to the tent flap and shoved him outside.

    The interior guard approached. "What's going on?" he asked.

    "We have a man here who's trying to kill us."

    Sergeant Morton arrived. "I want this man out of the tent," I said.

    "All right, Kestner, Calm down."

    "He wants us all dead."

    "I'll take him to the tool tent. You calm down."

    After breakfast next morning, Sergeant Morton called me into his tent. The offender, a new Pfc. only a week or so in first squad, had protested to Lieutenant Smith.

    "I know it was stupid," I said. "It's just that he placed the whole squad in jeopardy."

    "You were justified in some kind of disciplinary action," Morton said. "But not the zero tolerance leadership you showed in front of your men. Do you know that I could relieve you as squad leader?"

    "I regret turning him over and slamming him against the tent pole. I won't do that anymore."

    "See that you don't."

    I never made that mistake again, but I made others. Still, men requested transfer to first squad. We had a high survival rate.

    It was nearly summer. We worked in fatigues and slept in underwear beneath mosquito netting. After ten hours of road work, we'd settle in, lights out, the siren would sound, and here would come Bed Check Charlie. I'd zip down my netting, slide my feet into my boots, and take position behind the fifty caliber outside first squad tent, still in my long johns. Here would come the thrum of the engine, I'd try to aim by sound, and squeeze off intermittent bursts. Once a night, as predictable as the wail of an ambulance through a modern city, we would have our little chess game, always sometime between lights out and midnight.

Several times that month, the Chinese and North Koreans launched sudden offensives. We would break camp and head south in a routine as familiar as rush-hour. Each retrograde movement created long convoys, traffic jams, and pile-ups.

At the end of June, we were pulling back toward Uijonbju in a dust cloud and Sgt. Morton came back to D-21 and said that Lt. Smith and a Captain from Battalion needed to use her. I carried my M-1 and my bag of demolitions back to the last truck in the company convoy and settled down alone on a tent. Behind us was an infantry battalion, bouncing along at the same slow pace. We'd grind along 200 yards and stop to let the dust catch up and cover us.

From the hills behind us, there was occasional artillery fire, but it was rare when one landed close. On both sides of the road, the paddies were green with young rice plants. There was a thin parchment of dust on everything close to the road.

The truck lurched forward in first gear, stopped, lurched, and stopped again right beside a honey hole festering in the heat. We sat there a long time, and the stench kept growing. Out of boredom, I guess, I reached into my demo bag and pulled out a pound block of TNT and screwed in a detonator with a 15 second delay. The truck lurched forward again, I pulled the pin, and tossed the TNT into the honey hole.

Behind us, the infantry commander, a Lieutenant Colonel, was standing in his jeep with his head and shoulders above the windshield. We were about thirty feet away from the sweltering honey hole when the TNT detonated with a whoom sending a plume of foul brown water flying straight up into the air. It spread as it came down, landing with a first sploosh followed by random splatters all over the Colonel's jeep.

"Incoming! Incoming!" someone yelled, and behind the colonel, his infantry troops dismounted from their trucks, hunting for shelter in low spots alongside the road. I locked my demo bag in the Platoon tool box in a hurry, jumped from the truck, and took shelter alongside the road. But I watched under my arm as the Colonel wet a kerchief with water from a canteen and began wiping carefully sidewise from the bridge of his nose, away from each of his eyes, one after the other, flipping the handkerchief and wringing it dry between each wipe. The driver turned on the wiper blades, smearing half-moons in the caramel-colored sludge. When the trucks began to advance, I ran to jump in the back, hoping I would still have my stripes tomorrow.

Chapter 10:

JOHNNY

We moved north again, in one of our endless yo-yo patterns, up and down, sidewise, and backwards across the Chorwon Valley. At the end of June, first squad was on a long-range security patrol and came late in the afternoon to a small, still-smoking village the enemy had raided. There were three or four burned-out huts in a valley with terraced rice paddies alongside a creek.

It seemed a pleasant place to live. The view lingered for miles down hills and across the valley. There was green foilage now, the heart of summer, and the air hummed with insects. On two sides, the arms of the hills enfolded the village, and behind the hills, the blue mountains gazed, serene and untroubled, toward the distant Yellow Sea.

The Chinese had withdrawn when we approached. We surrounded the village, and while a flank patrol covered us, Davies and I scratched through the debris without luck for survivors. I made a note to alert the Quartermaster Corps to have the Graves Registration unit bury and make a record of the bodies.

From the hillside, I noticed a young boy walking toward us. His feet were bare and he was dressed only in a thin shirt and short pants. Talley and High Pockets were covering him. The boy walked straight up to me. "OK, GI," he said.

"You're pretty gutsy," I said. "Where are your parents?"

He shrugged.

"Mama?" I asked.

He looked over at the bodies.

"I'm sorry. Some people will come to bury them. You come with me, ok?" I translated as much as I could with my hands.

"OK."

Captain Kulbes said he could stay in the 2nd Platoon's headquarters tent and eat at the company mess. The men in the company found clothes and shoes that fit more or less, and he became the youngest and smallest of Kulbes' Mongrels. I named him Johnny, after a kid I knew back home.

We were back at our on-again, off-again camp on the south bank of the Imjin. The water in the river was low. The air buzzed with mosquitoes, flies and

Johnny lived in 2nd Platoon Headquarters tent.

59

millers. We bathed in the river after work details or screening patrols. Johnny stayed in camp, policing the tent and arranging with the Korean women who showed up each day to do our laundry. He sometimes tagged along after Leland Lipscomb. Libscomb served as the carpenter for the platoon and the company. He later did special assignments for the Battalion.

I spanked Johhny once for hitting a Korean laundrywoman, but except for that incident, he quickly adapted to first squad's daily routine. He followed behind us to chow and hung out after dinner in the tent until someone remembered that he was a growing boy, and growled that it was sacktime.

He became the company shoe-shine boy. I wore russet type buckle boots that didn't need shining. "You have number ten boots," Johnny would say, "No can shine."

"It's ok," I'd reply, "I like Johnny anyway."

"No. You get number one boots, and Johnny shine."

News of truce talks in the Stars and Stripes was demoralizing, coming along just when we were about to win the war. The feeling that we were on the verge of winning the war is one I should have suspected; we had seemed on the verge of winning from the moment we had landed, in October, 1950. In fact, that campaign had been named the Home-by-Christmas Offensive. We had seemed on the verge of winning the war just before the chinese launched their devastating May Day Offensive, and here we seemed on the verge of winning for a third time. That's all a soldier wants...to win the war.

But we were adrenalin-pumped. We blamed Truman for initiating peace talks just when we had won our way clear to victory. Soon his name began to drift through the air like a mosquito, usually accompanied by a string of off-color adjectives describing his sexual practices or his questionable family lineage. After morning chow on June 29th, we were called to attention by the first Sergeant.

"Gentlemen, the commander wants a word with the company."

Captain Kulbes mounted the front bumper of his jeep like he always did. He read from the Uniform Code of Military Justice and gave us another little talk about not speaking out against the President or the U.S. Congress. The next man who spoke out against the President would be court-martialed. It was much like the little talk we had after MacArthur was fired. And yet, there was a kicker. Beer rations were going to be cut due to a request by Eleanor Roosevelt. She was upset by the behavior of some drunken soldiers in San Francisco. I wasn't a beer drinker, but I put her name on my list a second time out of sympathy for Sergeant Morton and the other two-hundred-and-fifty thousand beer-meisters in Korea.

Funny. They can pull a grown man out of his life, troop him half-way around the globe, and order him to kill in the most methodical, cold-blooded ways imaginable. We didn't call it killing. There are euphemisms like "pile-driving" or "tomahawking" that substitute for "killing". And then, when one of these men is safely out of the war, at last, and has too much to drink, it makes Mrs. Roosevelt so uncomfortable that beer rations are cut off for a whole Army. Captain Kulbes was right. There was nothing democratic about it.

First squad mounted another long range patrol that day, tramping without incident until the early afternoon. On our return round, we came to a small ridge and, seeing movement, I signalled an Alert. I raised my head above the high grass that was musty with the smell of summer, and watched over the sights of my M-1 until I saw the movement again. It was a Mongolian pony, grazing, in the rich meadow below us. We fanned out and approached. (You can't be too cautious with a pony.) He'd been abandoned or lost by a Chinese unit; there was a scabbed-over bullet wound across his rump.

"Kestner, you're a farm boy," Lafonte said. "What do these things do? Do they give milk?"

"The Chinese probably used him to carry supplies."

"Shall we shoot him?"

"He's Chinese. We'll take him prisoner."

I proceeded to mount after fashioning a bridle and harness out of tent rope. I rode back into camp with the whole squad marching behind me. The entire company turned out, like they'd never seen a horse. I rode to the orderly room door and dismounted when the first sergeant appeared.

"First Sergeant, 1st Squad, 2nd Platoon reporting in from patrol. All is well. We captured one Chinese, slightly wounded."

"Kestner, what are we going to do with a damn pony?"

"He's a Communist, Sarge. He's a prisoner of war."

Tom Ortega, who had been watching, called me Pancho Villa with his Mongolian steed. The Quartermaster from another unit asked for him, and I had to go after dinner and show them how to lead him into a trailer.

My stomach acted up that night and continued for the next few days. On July 4, I couldn't eat breakfast. I should have known something was wrong then because I couldn't remember the last time that I passed up a meal.

We set out on a long-range patrol over Papa-san mountain. On top of a hill, we found troop fires, still smoldering, near a monastery, but no enemy. By noon, I was in bad shape. The idea of eating made me want to throw up. Talley asked if he could carry me. Fat chance. He asks if we should cancel the patrol. Another fat chance. He must have forgotten he was talking to a tough guy.

That afternoon was a blur of mosquitoes, glaring sun and small hills that grew steeper while I climbed them. The pain spread like a razor cutting through my chest. Talley hung close the whole afternoon, and when we finally returned to camp, he walked with me to report to the first sergeant. Captain Kulbes was standing there, I remember, just as the ground rose up and smashed me in the face.

Chapter 11:

THE DARK ON ME

I look up into the spinning blades of a helicopter. I don't know why it is here. High Pockets and Talley are here, for some reason. There is something I need to tell them, but I've forgotten what it is.

Days or weeks go by. I am in a tent with my Grandfather. At the other end of the tent, a man is stretched out on a table. Grandpa looks at the man on the table and says something to me. I know it's important and I strain to understand, but it's in a language I've never heard before. Finally I understand that I'm the man on the table. I'm lying on the table, staring at the underside of a canvas tent. Without turning my head to look, I can see myself and my grandfather, who are at the other end of the tent. They are talking now, but I can't hear what they say. Above me, there are bright lights. They've always been there. I can almost make out what they mean.

Nurse Rainor was reading The Naked and the Dead. She looked over at the soldier and seeing that he was awake, said "Welcome back".

"What's wrong?"

"You had a burst appendix. We had to operate." She set down her book and pulled the sheet away in order to dress my wound.

"Don't do that," I protested while reaching for the sheet to cover myself. A razor blade slashed my groin open. I collapsed back and she continued to fiddle around down there in a department where I'm admittedly shy. "What do you think you are doing?" I contested.

"I have to medicate you," she said. She pushed my hips upright and gave me a shot in the cheek of the butt, then slowly let me down onto my back. She resumes her little project down there where she's uninvited.

"What are you doing now?"

"I have to dress your wound."

"What kind of wound?"

"You have holes for the tubes. We have to drain you."

"I'm not used to girls looking at me. Isn't there a male nurse around?"

"I've seen what you have. I have to dress your wound."

The shot of morphine drifts in and nothing seems very important anymore. A male doctor appears and watches for a moment. "It's good to see him out of his coma," he says.

"What's the date?" I ask. They both turn to look at me. "It's July 7th," the nurse answers.

I remember that it's important to know the date for some reason. The nurse turns to the doctor. "They must not have any women wherever he grew up," she says. "He made a total fuss when I started to dress him."

I needed to get back to the squad. An appendix wasn't very serious, I was pretty sure, but I didn't know about a coma. I would ask them about it later.

I came home one afternoon and my parents had moved out, hahaha. It's a retreaded, second-rate joke, the sort you hear in a floor show at one of the cheesier Las Vegas casinoes. I was nine, and we were living a couple of miles outside of Anniston in a two-room house surrounded by summer cotton. As usual, my dad wasn't getting along with the farmer he was share-cropping for. I knew that we might be thrown out of the house, but I went to town anyway, hoping to mow a lawn or two.

Sure enough, the house was empty by the time I returned. I gathered my things up and tied them inside a towsack. I knew the railroad track ran in a straight shot, Anniston to East Prairie, where my grandpa lived, but my bike would never stand up for that kind of rough riding. I decided to ride back through Anniston, then two or three miles out of the way, to Highway 105, where the road was better, and from there up to my grandfather's house.

I had hiked the backwoods most of the winter picking wild pecans. I sold them for eight cents a pound at the general store so I could buy the bike. It was a stout, old Schwinn, but it had passed through a lot of owners and taken a lot of abuse. The fenders and handle-bar grips were missing and a torn piece of cracked leather partially covered the metal saddle. Worse still, each tire slowly leaked air. With the towsack and tire pump awkwardly balanced across the handlebars, I began, stopping twice before I even reached Anniston to pump air into the tires, and once again before I reached Highway 105, just after sunset. A knob appeared on the rear tire, and I pedaled each stroke thinking it might be my last.

The towsack got more unwieldy the farther I went, and I had to lean over the handlebars to hold it in place with one hand while I steered with the other. Without a reflector, the highway was dangerous at night and whenever headlights approached, I pulled over and waited until the car had passed. Three or four long, slow, miles along the highway, I passed an old barn with a water pump out front. I pulled into the yard, pushed the bike under a side shed, leaned it against the side, and walked out front to the pump, thinking how good cold water would taste.

But the pump had been dismantled, and it made me thirstier than before. I walked back to the shed and sat beside my bike. I didn't cry, men don't cry, but I was tired and hungry. I stretched out on the ground and closed my eyes.

A man with a black dog began yelling at me, calling me a thief. I told him I was going to my grandpa's house in East Prairie and only stopped for water. He told me the pump didn't even work. I said I knew that, now. I was just resting. He said he would let the sheriff decide what I was up to and told me not to move and walked away toward the hog pens.

I ran around the barn away from him, in a straight shot through a weedy side-yard toward the woods. Just before I reached the first trees, the man sicked his dog after me. I ran with my head down to avoid branches, heading toward the railroad tracks a hundred yards away. I could hear the dog gaining rapidly on me.

There was a wide drainage ditch full of dark water beside the tracks. I waded across and ran beside the tracks. The dog stopped on his side of the ditch, barking and slavering. He ran a few yards ahead of me, stopped to bark and growl until I passed him, then ran to catch up and bark again. There was water and muck inside my one pair of shoes that squished with each step.

Ahead of us the ditch emptied into a large canal that the tracks crossed over on a trestle bridge. If the dog didn't cross the ditch before he came to the canal, he probably couldn't get across the canal. Water moccasins would kill him.

I started across the bridge, and the dog pulled up at the canal, barked, whined, retraced his steps, jumped into the small ditch and swam across. He shook himself and began to chase me again. I stopped at the top of the bridge and looked into the canal. Snakes swam on the surface in slow, lazy esses. Now, the dog was almost on me, his lips pulled back to expose his glinty pointed teeth, a gurgling growl coming from low in his throat.

I jumped.

The splash of my entry startled the snakes swimming around under the bridge. I swam downstream as fast as I could. The dog barked without stop, approached the edge of the bridge, looked over, whined, began barking again. A snake swam toward me. I splashed at him and was surprised that he swam away.

The banks of the canal grew steeper, and when I looked back, I could no longer see the bridge. I knew the canal was dammed by a levee at the Mississippi and drained into the river through an underwater pipe taller than I was that would suck me under. I had to find a way out, but the current was speeding up. I began to back-pedal. I swam toward the bank, drifted under a willow, and grabbed a branch. It held a moment and then broke. I drifted with the current, thinking how ordinary it was to die, and staring eye to eye at Water Mocassins stretched out on the bank.

I was carried by the increasing current around a bend and away from the bank, past a spot where a rotten old tree lay half-in and half-out of the water. I put my head down and swam for it. A Cotton Mouth hissed at me as I approached. I splashed him and he slipped into the water. I crawled onto the trunk, then up the bank, and down the backside, tumbling on my hands and knees into a corn-field, murmuring in a soft night breeze. The image was just so tranquil, like there had never been a speck of trouble in the history of the world.

I lay on my back a long time, then picked a few ears of green corn which I chewed one hard kernel at a time while I followed the levee to the end of the corn field. From there, I headed in the direction I guessed was East Prairie, through a patch of thorny blackberry vines and horse weeds, toward some woods. I drank water from a small ditch, gritty and smelly, but thirst-quenching.

I sat against a tree and fell asleep. I woke up when raccoons riffled my overalls, stealing my corn. I shooed them away and just sat there until I slept again.

A downpour startled me from sleep. Lightning flared, lighting up the woods. The thunder shook the branches. I started walking. I cupped my hands to gather rainwater and caught enough to remind me how thirsty I was.

The rain stopped and before long, it grew hot. It wasn't soon enough when I heard the afternoon train headed for East Prairie and ran, hoping to catch it. It was nowhere in sight.

I followed the tracks. The scratches from the blackberry bushes began to itch and burn with sweat. I had blisters from my wet shoes. Ahead of me, at a dirt road across the tracks, cars and pickups stopped. Men with rifles got out of the vehicles and began firing at me. I ran into the trees.

I was a wanted criminal. The injustice of it finally got to me. Not only had I not stolen anything, the farmer now had everything I owned, and the sheriff was chasing me. It was no way to treat a nine year old.

I stayed behind a large oak until it got dark and the shots finally stopped. If I followed the tracks, they could still capture me. I headed back the way I came, through the woods, toward the sound of passing cars that I figured was Highway 105.

It was nearly midnight when I turned from the center of East Prairie onto South Martin Street and headed to the government project housing where grandpa lived. When I got to the last block before his house, I ran without stopping until I reached his porch and stood there a minute letting it sink in that I was safe before I knocked repeatedly on the front door.

When nobody answered, I tapped at all the windows, and when there was still no answer, I began to search for one that was unlocked. I was more hungry, more tired and more lonely than I had ever been before. I pumped water into a tin cup that always hung beside the pump and drank until I sloshed, then filled the cup again and poured it over me, clothes and all. The light next door came on, the front door opened, and a flashlight shined in my eyes.

"Frankie!" Mr Watson said. "What are you doing here in the middle of the night?"

"Where's my grandpa?"

"Your aunt's having a baby. They'll be back this morning, I expect." He walked closer. "You look like you've been through the wringer, son. What happened?"

"Well, my folks are separated again and I came to stay with grandpa. It was dark on me and I stayed in this barn and the farmer came and said he would throw me in jail and I ran away and he sicked his dog on me and I swam in a drainage canal to get away. I didn't steal anything. Some men started shooting at me."

"Slow down," Mr Watson said. "Are you hungry?"

"Yes, sir."

We walked back to his house, where Mrs. Watson cooked eggs and bacon to go with some left-over biscuits that I ate with sorghum. Ah! I thanked her, stretched out on the floor in the living room and slept.

The chaplain was sitting beside me, praying, when I woke. He asked how I was feeling. "A little sore," I said. "Where am I?"

"Uijongbu," he answered. "You've been under for, let's see, four days now. But the doctor says you're going to make it."

"I thought I just had an appendix removed."

"Yours burst," he said. "You're lucky to be alive."

I had been insolent to the Chaplain the last time I saw him, at Pusan. Eleanor Roosevelt had led a successful campaign to have all soldiers under the age of eighteen returned home, and against my wishes, the Chaplain had pushed through orders for me to be relieved of active duty. I felt that leaving in the middle of a war would be a kind of betrayal of my company. Besides, I didn't want to go home. back to share cropping and the kind of life I'd had before I joined the Army. I'd called him about a hundred kinds of names.

I remembered how he had tried to get me shipped home, back at Pusan, out of kindness, and I'd called him about a hundred kind of names. "You know what?" I asked. "I know how mean I was to you back at Pusan. I want to apologize."

"Your apology is accepted, Corporal. But don't worry about that. You just get well."

The nurse came in. The Chaplain stood up and asked her to keep him posted on my condition. When he had left, the nurse pulled the sheet back, exposing me to the world, then turned me on my side and gave me another shot of morphine.

It took about one minute for it to not matter a bit who saw me. I watched the ceiling of the tent rise and fall in the breeze. My body became as light as a thought, and I floated up to the ceiling of the tent. It's easy enough. You have to try without trying at all.

It was still dark when I woke. I ate cold biscuits with pork back while I fried up and made two egg sandwiches. It was summer, I'd already helped Dad weed his twenty acres, and had settled in to wait for the next weeding when I heard that a farmer outside of Dorena was looking for cotton choppers. He was cantankerous and nobody would work for him and he stood to lose most of his cotton, so he wasn't too picky about who he hired, even a fourteen-year old kid who showed up alone. I rode down on my bike, arriving while it was still dark, and waited for the farmer outside his barn.

It's comforting to watch a farm house wake up. One first rooster creaks out an unconfident crow. Then, he's quiet again, like he thinks he's made a mistake. But no, it's morning all right, he can feel it, taste it in the air. His second crow is more confident: "It's morning. I know now that it's morning." Baby birds begin to chirp and soon the treetops are a ceaseless orchestra of whistles, trills, and tweets.

A yellow light comes on in a bedroom, and after a minute, you hear a toilet flush. The dog on the porch pushes himself up, stretches, turns around a few times, and collapses back in his former spot. The kitchen light snaps on, casting a faint light onto the driveway.

The rooster decides he had it right the first time and he crows again, in throaty assurance: "See? I told you. It's morning." The stock animals begin to mill around, clamoring for breakfast in a hundred mooes and squeaks, quacks, clucks, grunts, whinnies, whistles, clicks, and snorts.

The smell of coffee drifts across the yard, followed immediately by the sharp tang of bacon. The dog raises himself on his front paws, his nostrils flared wide. He barks at a sudden pack of wolves who have invaded the yard and threaten the stock animals.

The front door opens and the farmer steps out, dressed in coveralls and a t-shirt. "Did you get 'em, Jonesie?" he asks and bends over to scratch his fearless guardian behind the ears. He straightens, pushes his hands deep into his coveralls, and looks both ways up the dirt road.

"Breakfast is ready!" comes a yell from inside the house. The farmer spits into the yard, scratches Jonesie once more behind the ears and goes inside.

The headlights of a pickup bounce up the road. At the driveway, it turns in, and parks. I can't believe it for a minute, Evelyn and Treva Sutton, dressed for work, in long sleeve shirts and jeans, carrying cotton gloves and straw hats, step down on the other side. They say goodbye to their dad. My throat freezes up and I don't remember how to stand and my hands stick out.

Hi, Treva. Isn't it a great morning? Do you want to go to a movie after work? Oh, that's ok. How about Saturday night? Good. I'll meet you at the Dorena Theatre at five —I plan it out, analyze it, turn it this way and that, consider the options, take her point of view into consideration. I don't say word number one.

"Hi, Frank," Evelyn says.

"Oh, Hi." That's great. Like I didn't even see her standing there before. "Hi, Treva."

"Morning, Franklin!"

Easy. This talking to girls business is easy. Like flying, you have to try without trying at all.

I got the job, at adult wages, and worked the rest of the week with the Suttons and a few other hands. On Saturday night, I met my friend Slewfoot at the Dorena and bragged that I'd spent the week chopping cotton with the Sutton girls.

"Did you talk to 'em?"

"Sure did."

"What did they say back?"

"Not much, Slew. We were busy working."

"I bet you didn't say more than two words."

"I did too."

I said four words. Then I waited all week for my next opportunity. When the fields were chopped, late Friday, we even stood around together outside the barn for a few minutes, waiting to be paid.

It was my last chance, and I squirmed on the inside, trying to think of what I could say. When the Sutton girls were paid, they chatted with the farmer like it was any old Friday, and it was the opportunity I'd been waiting for, to talk about the weather or the condition of the cotton or the mosquitoes. Then I could ask Treva about that movie. But I had rooted into the ground like a beet and watched them walk away from me, toward their truck, across a distance that grew wider the more I wanted to cross it, and my voice became hypothetical, a complicated possibility, like the sound of water deep in an underground cave, where it was easy to lose yourself trying to find its source.

I climbed back up and out of the cave. Maybe, a minute had passed...or an hour...it may have been a different day altogether. I didn't recognize the nurse who was taking my pulse rate. There were lamps and night shadows in the tent. I asked when I could get back to my company.

"You're not going back to your company for several weeks."

"I heard an appendix isn't too serious."

"Well, soldier, you let yours burst and got gangrene. You nearly died. The doctors worked really hard to clean you up." Then she jerked the covers off, exposing me, turning me over, and shooting me up.

When I woke again, Nurse Rainor was sitting beside me with a bowl of bouillon soup. She raised my head and lifted a spoon to my mouth.

"Nurse, I can feed myself."

"No you can't. You have needles in your arms." She raised my head enough that I could see the needles and the draining tubes that came out of my stomach and dripped a foul liquid into a large bottle. She wiped around my mouth with a napkin. Some tough Combat Engineer, splayed apart and formless as a baby bird, while a wisp of a woman held my head and spoon-fed me.

On July 9th, they dressed me for a helicopter ride to the 121st Evacuation Field Hospital at Kimpo. It was the first time that I had my drawers on for a long time. From the air, I could see all the roads I helped build and the places where I had fought, the bridge over the Han, and the whole city of Seoul. There was block after block of masonry debris and burnt out artillery scars.

At Kimpo, they carried me from the helicopter straight inside a tent to a hospital bed. A doctor appeared and gave me a shot of morphine in the same sore, red cheek as all the other shots. It stung, but he was a man, and he only lowered my drawers.

Two days later, they loaded me onto a C-54 bound for Taegu with guys who were missing arms and legs and I felt like I was cheating. At the 155th Field Hospital, I got the urge to go to the bathroom, but I didn't say anything because I didn't want to use a bed pan. Finally, the urge was irresistable, and I told the nurse.

"They took the stitches out yesterday," she said. "We can go, but we have to be careful."

"We?"

"That's right, soldier. One little slip and you could open your wound." She helped me sit up, then raised my arm over her shoulder and lifted, and pretty soon here goes leader of men and all around tough guy, Corporal Kestner, aka Little Caesar, being carried on the shoulders of a woman nurse who couldn't weigh a hundred-twenty-five, down to the bathroom to make doo-doo. She even went inside with me to help me seat myself and then stood there... waiting.

"I don't think I can go with you in the room," I said.

"I'll wait right outside the door. You call as soon as you've finished. Don't try to stand by yourself."

It was July 12 and if my personal battles were included in the headlines from the Korean War for that date, it might read like this:

AT KAESONG, PEACE TALKS ENTER THIRD DAY.

WAR-WEARY SOLDIERS HOLD LINE AT 38th PARALLEL.

RIDGWAY DOUBTS SPEEDY END TO HOSTILITIES.

AT TAEGU, CORPORAL KESTNER DOES NUMBER TWO.

Chapter 12:

HIGH TOWER

At midnight, on September 5, 1941, my grandfather, Hightower Morland had set himself down on the railroad tracks outside of Lilbourn, Missouri, and began to sing a Cherokee lament that he had known all his life. He had a bottle of whiskey and more American history than he could stomach.

The freight train passed our house in town, and I woke in a sweat, bed covers twisted around my legs, panting. My mother told me I had a nightmare, is all.

Hightower Morland's story, which ended abruptly that night, had begun a centry earlier, in Georgia. At that time, the Cherokee were successful and prosperous. They were an independent nation, with a constitution modeled after the U.S. Constitution, an elected principal chief, a senate, and a house of representatives. Sequoyah had created a Cherokee alphabet, they kept independent historical records, and even published a newspaper.

When gold was discovered on tribal lands, the state of Georgia issued an order for removal, using a document of agreement that no Cherokee recognized as having ever seen before, much less signed. The tribe initiated a counter suit, and the U.S.Supreme Court upheld their case. In Georgia, Judge Augustine nonetheless signed a removal order by military force, and President Andrew Jackson rejected a petition to intervene. Thousands died on the Long Walk to the Indian Territory in Oklahoma, where the remaining members joined the Five Civilized Tribes.

Like many of the others, Hightower's parents were unhappy on the new reservation, so unlike their tribal lands. With their new baby, they struck out on their own, finally settling on a little farm near the confluence of the Arkansas River and Mississpppi River. The land supported lots of game so they farmed, hunted, fished the rivers, and after a few years, began to raise ponies for sale.

When my grandfather was eleven, river pirates raided their homestead. Hidden by his mother under the wooden floor, Hightower had to listen, helplessly, as his mother and father were murdered. In the morning, he began his own long walk, back to the reservation, hoping they would take him in, singing the Cherokee songs that he had learned when he learned to talk.

He stopped at a white house to ask for food. The white people took him to the white sheriff, and he was taken to a white orphanage in Little Rock, Arkansas.

Orphanages are a modern invention of white Europeans dating from the same time that child labor became a common practice, and it's no accident that they share a similar attitude toward their wards. For a boy used to accompanying his father on his trapping and fishing rounds, the high fenced yard and locked doors of the orphanage became a prison. Grandfather was expected to pay his way by working long daily hours on the orphanage farm or on piece work and laboring jobs contracted by the orphanage. There were irregular lessons in English, which he found ugly and guttural, and never really mastered.

There was a Jewish girl at the orphanage, equally ostracized, though undistinguishable to my grandfather's way of seeing from the other white girls. Mary Schneider, my grandmother-to-be, and Hightower became friends almost by default. They were regulars, too old for adoption. They grew wise in the systems of surveillance, and skilled at finding time to talk together. In hand-written notes and brief conversations, they learned each other's story.

Mary's father, Gunther Schneider, had been a nobleman serving as German Attaché to Czechoslovakia. In the course of a bout with the flu, he met Mary's mother, who was a trained nurse working in the hospital against the wishes of her strictly Orthodox Jewish parents. They began to see one another after he had left the hospital, and in time, when they announced their intentions to marry, were disowned by their families.

They purchased forged documents, married secretly, and emigrated to America, eventually winding up in Memphis, where Mary's mother worked in a hospital and her father began a grocery, The Corner Store, at State and First Street. They bought a two-story frame house for eight hundred dollars and that served as Mary's birthplace. Her mother stayed home after the birth and they got by on the small earnings from the grocery. In 1888, first Mary's father, then her mother died of the flu, and she was passed along a chain of relief organizations until she landed in the Little Rock Orphanage.

They were on a picnic at Sulphur Springs when Hightower first heard Mary's story. They had slipped away to sit among some oaks on a small hill from which they could watch the caretakers and children playing baseball. Hightower couldn't think of anything to say except, I'm sorry.

"It just happened," Mary said. She plucked a stem of grass and began pulling it apart. "Hightower is a funny name," she said, after a minute. "How did you get that name?"

"My mother," Hightower said. "She said I could climb a tree like squirrel, so she gave me that for an English name."

"You need a second name in English. Do you have one?"

"No."

"Can I give you one?"

"OK, I guess. Sure."

"Let me see.... How about Washington or Lincoln?"

"Like the Presidents?"

"Sure. Start at the top."

"I don't want to be president."

"OK." She put down the stalk she had twisted apart, turned her head to one side and closed her eyes, concentrating. "Morland," she said. "That's English enough, and it's hopeful, too."

"How does Mrs. Morland sound?" Hightower asked.

"I think it sounds lovely," Mary said.

"Would you like it for your name?"

"Why Mr. Morland," she said. "I do believe you are proposing to me."

"Yes, ma'am."

"Well, Mr. Morland, I'd be delighted."

"First, we got to get away from this place," Hightower said.

It happened during the chaos of a late summer storm, with chickens frantically running everywhere and squealing pigs loose in the garden. While everybody else ran around desperately to catch livestock, Hightower and Mary gathered their few possessions. Hightower took the keys from the desk in the lobby, opened the wide front doors, and they walked away, free, into the wide world before them.

For the next weeks they lived in the woods, staying off the roads and away from towns and villages. Autumn made the nights cold. They lived in a cave for weeks, while Hightower caught beaver and sold pelts. Dressed in warm new store-bought clothes, they crossed the Mississippi on a ferry and headed south, ahead of the coming winter.

They married and learned to sharecrop in a small town in the cotton belt while the seasons rolled by. Winters, Hightower continued to hunt and trap, selling the pelts. They saved their money and bought a wooded homestead with a house that had glass windows, and they multiplied. Eventually, there were a dozen: Mary and Hite, as she had begun to call him, their six boys and four girls.

They eventually purchased another farm and hired farmhands. They bought a tractor. They bought a four door Ford and bounced along the corduroy back roads to church or shopping or a movie. They were the Morlands, a prominent family, with houses and lands and cars and money in the bank. Their children began to marry and move away.

In 1929, the money in the bank vanished. Crop prices tumbled. Hightower became bitter. He had forgotten how deceptive white people were. He began to drink. It was during prohibition and whiskey was expensive, so he set up stills in the backwoods.

When he was arrested, he became a No-Speak Injun, refusing to name his partners in the whiskey business. He was convicted of Bootlegging and spent three years on the chain gang.

The farm slipped away. He drank more.

He returned to the reservation, completing the trip he had begun after the death of his parents. Mary refused to go with him, and he split his time between the reservation and Lilbourn. In August, 1941, he returned after learning that Mary was dying. My grandmother passed away in August of 1941, Hightower sat a whole day beside her grave, chanting his familiar songs. For the next week, he refused to enter her house and slept outside on the ground in spite of the fact the entire family was gathered there. Grandfather and I sat outside the house after one of our country dinners...the kind with more than you can eat, and more after that, leaving you happy to sag into a chair and lean against the side of the house like a bear settling into his cave. We were immobile but content, still savoring the rich varieties of tastes and aromas. My aunts and uncles came and went, cleaning up the dishes, or taking some air. Grandpa and I lolled in our chairs and he told me this story and made me promise that I would never drink alcohol.

Five days later, he set himself down on the railroad tracks and began to sing. The newspaper called it an accident.

KULBES' MONGRELS

Pfc. Thomas Ortega, 3d Plt.

Cpl. Kestner and Pfc. Lafonte.

The mongrel's moving up front.

Pfc. Raymond A. "Smitty" Smith, 3d Plt.

"Cookie" in the mess truck.

Cpl. Kestner in the spring of 1951, 50mg for Bed Check Charlie.

"The Blood Hounds", 1st Squad, 2nd Platoon Company D, 10th Combat Engineering.

New mongrels joining the company, with Cpl. Larry Lindgren.

Pvt. Leland Lipscomb, 1st Squad. With captured Burp gun.

Left to right: Private Eugene Florek, Pfc. Peter Talley, Sgt. Franklin Kestner.

Sgt. Franklin Kestner with 2nd Platoon Sgt. Pete Endersbee.

PFC Walter Piper, 1st Squad, Iowa.

Pvt. Walker outpost guard northwest of Yonchon with B.A.R.

PFC Walter Piper with Cpl. Peter Talley.

Cpl. Jack Bishop, 1st Squad.

Private E.L. "Highpockets" Wilkinson leaning on D-21 truck that is riddled with more than 170 bullet holes after combat at Chosin.

Corporal Thomas L. Ortega taking his weekly bath, hoping for a pass.

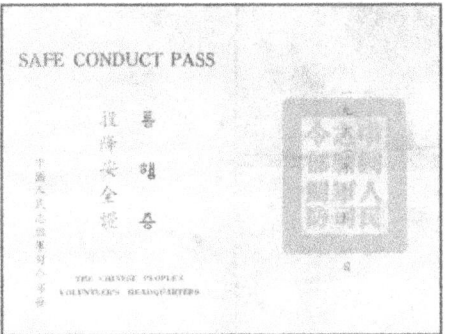
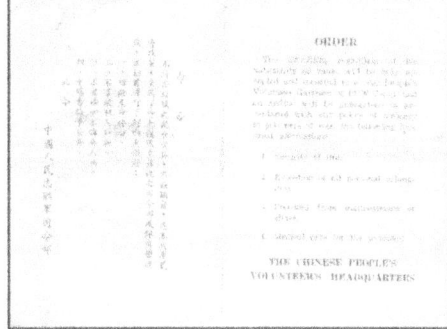
Chinese Good Conduct Pass, provided by Cpl. Thomas Ortega.

ALL IN A DAY'S WORK

Scout south of the Han River.

Photo of a Beach landing in North Korea, 1950.

Forward with the Infantry, 1951.

Moving up the Chorwon with the tanks.

Artillery set up possibly at Wonju.

Troops out in front of tanks.

WANTED: DEAD OR ALIVE

The Chinese could not hide from the F80s.

Napalm! The Chinese could not escape it!

The fate of American POWs at the hands of retreating North Koreans.

A lone dead Chinese killed by air strike.

The Chinese gave up in Hordes.

A lone Chinese POW found wandering lost.

A lone Chinese killed by air strike, February, 1951.

The Imjim River after the mayhem. The Mongrels leave.

SIGNS OF WAR

One of our men reading the sign.

Forward movement checked, Division Headquarters wants a sign. PFC Leland Lipscomb and Sgt. Ramon Cruz, D Company, 10th Engineers, accommodate; 24 January, 1952. (National Archives)

BATTLING THE ELEMENTS

It rained a lot in the spring of 1951.

Company D building a floating bridge across the Han River.

Imjin River in flood at monsoon time, 1951.

Monsoon caused vehicles to get stuck. What a mess.

SEOUL

Bombed and shelled section of Seoul, Korea. This was taken while I was on a three day pass to Seoul for R&R. The pass was a reward for building a map case for Major William Allison, battalion commander to be used at division headquarters in the war room. Photos by Pfc. Lipscomb.

The Hwachon Reservoir Dam.

Seoul MPs at check point.

Chapter 13:

THE PEACE TREATY WITH JAPAN

At Taegu, almost ten years after my Grandfather died, I had hovered for days on the verge of my own death. For a while, with my life in the balance, it seemed to change everything. But I was eighteen years old. I grew stronger and the dark hallucinations faded. I began to resume my old attitudes. The doctor saw that I was past danger and reassigned me to rehabilitation in Japan. One morning, I was loaded onto a gurney and then into a C-54 for a flight across the sea of Japan.

After landing at the Tokyo airport, they put six of us in a bus with a Japanese driver who drove like a frustrated Kamikaze pilot on a secret mission to kill all of us. I mistakenly complained to the nurse, who gave me a lecture called "Understanding Cultural Differences". But I was right. He drove all the way to Camp Zama outside of Yokohama at about fifty, his siren roaring, IVs swaying on their stands, the nurses holding onto their caps.

They put me into a bed, and here comes Big Nurse with her howitzer needles and her iron rules. She's on the fast track to sixty, stout as an infantry sergeant, with a heavy starched uniform and thick creases that run from both sides of her nostrils down beside her mouth. She wears thick white make-up and bright red lipstick that seems garish and out of place. For a minute, she stands at the end of the bed without saying anything to me, reading a clip-board. Finally, she looks up. "This is my ward, Corporal," she begins, and hangs the clip-board at the foot of the bed. "As long as you're here, you'll do as you're told. There is to be no smoking in the ward. There is to be no foul language and no horse play. You will treat our Japanese staff with respect, got it?"

"Yes ma'am."

"All right Corporal. Expose a cheek."

I lifted my face.

"Are you a smart guy?"

"I don't know what you mean."

She slapped herself on the butt.

I turned and pulled down my pajamas.

She slammed a 155mm needle home with the kind of vigor that would make a field artillery commander proud. Welcome to Japan.

I drifted away, into the air.

When I woke up, a nurse led me to the dentist, a Japanese woman who had studied dentistry with the Marquis de Sade. She poked around in my mouth like she was trying to kill a snake. When she found a couple of cavities, she "aahhed" with great zeal, and began a reenactment of Pearl Harbor inside my mouth. She forced my mouth wide apart, pushed my tongue back, and started drilling. Enamel chips flew and blood flowed into my throat.

"Dot you hab eddy dobocaide?" I asked.

She pushed with still more force, a hard-rock miner on a production schedule. The air stunk of burnt enamel.

"Don't you have any novocaine?" I asked again, when she released my tongue.

"Small cavities. No use novocaine," she said. The drill whirred. "You number one baby-san," she said and dived back in, fully armed. She had opportunity, motive, and intent, your Honor. This was not a crime of passion. This was a premeditated, calculated assault, and I ask for the strongest penalty the court can impose.

She finally got tired, I think, and released me, still alive, but aching-jawed, my tongue drill-burnt, tasting blood and scorched tooth enamel, with tiny flecks of silver stuck in my palate like shrapnel.

I was recuperating in the ward when a Japanese orderly asked me to change chairs so he could mop, and I explained his Japanese lineage to him, from its early beginnings as slime mold up to and including his promiscuous mother and unknown father.

He nodded and bowed.

The Japanese were on my list. They'd spent the first half of the twentieth century raping and pillaging one country after another as far as I was concerned. We wouldn't even have been in Korea except that they had fastened on it like a leech for fifty years, then dropped it in shambles and disarray, a push-over for an invasion.

I wanted to march back into the dentist's office with an ax handle and demonstrate a technique of lightning-quick, novocaine-free tooth removal that might prove helpful to her career. The orderlies were involved in her secret war, I figured, and I let them know every chance I could exactly what I thought of them.

Pretty soon, here's Big Nurse taking a seat beside me in the cafeteria.

"You're going to have to change the way you talk to our Japanese staff," she says.

"I don't trust them."

"I don't give a damn."

"They don't think the war is over."

"Let me put it this way," she says. "I am not going to take any crap from a teen-age Corporal. You have an order to change your behavior from a Captain in the U.S. Army. If you want to keep your stripes, you'll change your attitude."

"I won't talk to them at all."

"See that you don't."

I was soon back on solid provisions. I could eat ground beef patties in dark gravy, mashed potatoes, bread, jello, and coffee. Things were looking up. I could go to the bathroom by myself and go to chow alone. I still didn't care for wearing those funny little britches that tie in the front... comfortable enough, but scantier than I like.

Finally, they issued me underclothes. I was provided two summer dress uniforms, a field uniform, low-quarters, not boots like I asked for, a tie and my brass. I also had a couple of shirts, with my Combat stripes hanging heavy on the arm: I felt my sense of power and authority return and yes, I could keep on my pants. I dressed and went to the barbershop for a crew-cut and came back to the ward where the guys oohed and aahed. One forlorn Pfc was the highest rank besides me. In war, it's the young men who fill up the hospitals.

"Hey Kestner," the ward sergeant said. "I didn't know you were a Corporal."

"Yeah, Sergeant. I've been a Corporal for a long time."

"You can't have been a corporal for too long. You're only eighteen years old."

"In Korean time, it's long."

The next day I started rehab with a Japanese therapist. I kept my mouth shut about it, and went through the drill, and we got along fine.

I was behind on my meals, thin and pale as a coal miner, and always hungry. I ate twice a day at the snack bar, in addition to my normal meals, always ordering a cheeseburger with fries and a Pepsi, and the girl who worked there got so she would start frying a patty as soon as she saw me. I was working on the last few fries one morning when the ward sergeant sat beside me with a cup of coffee.

"I've noticed you've gotten a lot friendlier with the Japanese staff," he said.

"Big Nurse," I said. "She gave me a little talking-to."

"Oh?" he said. "And that's it? Are you sure it doesn't have anything to do with Kimka?"

I ate my last french fry. "Who's that?"

"Oh, right!" he said. "Like you haven't noticed how she rushes over to serve you whenever you show up and starts spouting 'Corporal Kestners' all over the room like a parrot."

"Nope. I never noticed."

"She's a pretty girl."

"I suppose so." I stood up.

"You should take her to a movie or something."

"I've got a girl friend."

The days drifted by, and finally, on the first of August, they called me into the office and a headquarters sergeant told me I could go home.

"Home where?"

"The States."

"I want to go back to my division, my battalion, my company, and my squad."

"Are you kidding?"

"No, Sarge."

The sergeant sent me to the Captain.

"I left my squad, and I'm not finished with Korea," I said.

"It's fine with me."

"But I want to go back to my unit."

He cut the order right there. I went to the replacement unit, where I was the ranking man again. They put me on a day long train trip to Sasebo, where at just-dark, I boarded the Mori-Mori, an antique Japanese troop ship, with a lot of recruits going to Korea for the first time.

Sleeping quarters were a large, straw-matted floor below decks with little clusters of guys gambling, reading, talking, turning the air blue with cigarette smoke and curses. I dozed off and on until we docked the next afternoon at Pusan. Since I already had my unit assignment, they quickly dispensed with my paper work and put me in a room by myself. Some privates came in that night and we sat up late, talking about combat.

At formation the next morning, the sergeant told me I'd been AWOL and he was going to have my stripes.

"How could I be AWOL if I haven't gone anywhere?"

"We checked your room. How old are you anyway?"

"I spent most of the night in my room talking to the privates from next door. I'm eighteen, Sergeant."

I found the guys, and they backed up my story, but the sergeant wouldn't listen.

The two privates went with me to company headquarters, where I protested to the commander that the Charge of Quarters should be more responsible. The privates confirmed that we had been up late, talking.

"Why didn't you just clear this up with the CQ?" the Colonel asked.

"We tried. He wouldn't listen, sir."

The Captain said to his aide, "Get the CQ in here."

When the sergeant showed up, we were called back into the Captain's office and the matter was cleared up in a brief monologue that touched on the matter of losing one's stripes (no matter how many) in a hurry, and how being confronted unfairly could make a man rankle.

"Don't you think it's a pretty good policy if you're going to take a man's stripes to be damn sure that he's done what you said first?" the Captain asked.

"Yes sir," the sergeant answered.

"What do you think we should do about the Corporal's stripes, Sergeant?"

"Nothing, sir."

"Thank you, Sergeant. You men, thank you, too." We saluted and left, following behind the sergeant, who had nothing more to say to us at all. I was anxious, and at the train that night, I asked the replacement sergeant to sign my orders.

"I've never done that," he said.

"Well, do it for me."

The overnight train stopped for a long time in Taegu and, it was nine the next morning, before we pulled in to Seoul, where there was a 3d Division truck waiting. I found a 3rd Division sergeant and asked him to sign my orders.

"What's this for?"

"Well, I had a little trouble in Pusan, and I want to document where I've been."

He signed it. "I see you were on the Mori Mori," he said.

"That's right."

"It sank on its return to Japan."

The truck dropped me off at battalion headquarters, where I met the supply sergeant and waited until after noon for a ride to Dog Company, which was in a new camp only about half-a-mile from where we were when I left. I found Captain Kulbes alone in the command tent.

"Sir, Corporal Kestner reporting for duty, sir." I handed him my papers.

"Well, hello, Corporal Kestner," he said. He looked over the papers. "I never thought I'd see you again, but I'm glad to have you back. How are you feeling?"

"I'm ready for duty, sir."

"You've been in the hospital for more than four weeks. You can go back to your squad, but I want you to put yourself on light duty for a month."

"Yes, Sir!" I gave a crisp salute, turned sharply, and exited. I found first squad's tent, stashed my things, and went back to the supply tent, looking without luck for my potato sack, which held my gear and armaments.

The chaplain was waiting for me when I returned to the first squad tent and invited me to coffee at the company mess. He was glad to see me safely back, he said, and invited me to Sunday services whenever I could come. I thanked him and we chatted a bit, but I knew that the services were going to be really late if they waited for me to show up before they began. Any god that created this world needed to have his head examined.

Sweaty, tired, griping and whining like they were still at Pusan and had never faced combat together, first squad began to straggle in: Lafonte and a new guy, gabbing while they walked, Talley, slow-talking, pipe-smoking Sergeant Meters, Pace, Endersbee, Piper, Ronnie Smith, Florek. We were back-slapping and saying helloes when the new guys, Lipscomb and Vandersteldt, and, then, the fly in the ointment, Epps, raised the flap and looked in.

"Oh God, Little Caesar is back," Epps says, to the air or to the ground or to nobody, but to me, in particular.

"What are you doing here?" I ask.

"I'm in first squad, now."

"We're kind of a utility squad," Lafonte said. "We've had two different leaders while you were away."

"Yeah," Talley said. "We're the company grunts."

"We'll see about that," I say.

"Are you back in first squad?"

"There's my gear." I motion to my cot. "We'll see if things don't shape up a little. Do you know what happened to my potato sack?"

"Sergeant Morton burned it. He kept your things in a foot locker, though."

Then I look out the flap and what do I see? A new damn squad truck, with a new name, Flossy, painted on the hood.

"Where's old D-21?" I ask.

"The motor sergeant," Talley said. "Bishop told him she ran just fine, but he wouldn't listen.

"We're the company orphans," Florek said. "Nobody gives a diddly what we think."

"Where's Bishop?"

"Home and gone," Talley said. "Here's the new driver, Eusebius Fischer."

"Eusebius?" I asked.

"Eusebius," he answered, and we shook hands. "You can call me Fischer."

"And Flossy?"

"She's my girlfriend."

"It hasn't been too lucky to paint your girlfriend's name on the truck."

"We told him," Florek said. "He thinks he's immune."

"I'm not very superstitious," Fischer said.

I go around to see Sergeant Morton.

"Hey, Kid. I heard you were back. You feeling ok?"

"I'm good, Sarge. First squad is in disarray, though."

"The replacement squad leader got transferred after about three weeks," he said.

"Sergeant, the motor sergeant got rid of D-21."

"When did that happen?"

"I don't know. But the captain gave an order not to get rid of that truck."

So we go to see the captain. He calls the motor sergeant in.

"Sergeant, why did you turn that truck in?"

"Sir, Corporal Kestner was gone. I got a new truck."

"Did D-21 ever fail?"

"Not that I know of."

"I gave an order back in Pusan that D-21 was not to be turned in as long as it could perform its mission," the Captain said. "Corporal Kestner and Sergeant Morton are upset, and the squad doesn't like it either. You go find D-21 and report back to me."

The sergeant left in his jeep.

After chow, I hunted up High-Pockets and asked him where D-21 was.

"Kestner, nobody thought you were coming back."

"High-Pockets, you're a traitor."

"Nobody else would have come back. I don't know about you. You must have a head injury they didn't find."

The motor sergeant drove to division ordnance at Inchon and was gone until late that night. The next morning he shows up at my tent. He's an E-5, looking to make First Class.

"Kestner, I can't find your truck," he begins. "I've looked at every two-and-a-half ton truck between here and Inchon. I got you a brand-new truck. Look at it. Crank it up."

"Sergeant, that's not D-21. The Captain gave you an order not to scrap her. We took care of her. You never had to do anything, just leave her alone. I come back from the hospital, and she's been scrapped. I don't like it."

"Do you know what this means?"

"It means you're a traitor."

"No, it means I can lose my stripes. I have to go talk to Captain Kulbes."

"This is personal to me. I wouldn't have made it out of Hagaru except for that truck."

"It's going to be personal for me if I'm walking around here slick-sleeved," the sergeant said. "Look. I'll keep this truck purring. I'll gas it up every day. Will you tell the Captain that it's ok?"

"I'll ask the squad what they think. Why didn't you listen to Bishop?"

We painted over the bumper and the stenciled number of the new truck. Leland Lipscomb hand-printed a Gothic D-21 on her bumper. High-Pockets asked if he should shoot some holes in her?

We decided we should have a memorial service and that it would be fitting if the motor sergeant attended. With the sergeant in tow, we put our red scarves on and walked out into a meadow. We held our helmets over our hearts.

Lafonte stepped forward to give the eulogy: "Dearly Beloved, we are gathered in remembrance of old D-21. She was stout-hearted and sure-footed, patient in hardship and courageous in adversity. She was a little jealous, but we will miss her. Wherever her spirit may be, we lay her to rest..."

We formed up and gave her a three-round volley. RIP, old D-21, old life saver.

Chapter 14:

IN TROUBLE WITH THE DRAFT BOARD

Sergeant Morton enlisted out of Tennessee during World War II, and returned there after the war. He worked construction for a year, and then re-upped, out of boredom and frustration. It was during a long period of radical military down-sizing. He didn't make rank again until the Korean War.

Although he would have liked to be an officer, each passing year made that more unlikely. Still, he didn't sweat and whine about his condition or the state of the world or the injustice of it all. He became a peerless sergeant.

Almost as soon as I'd been assigned to the Engineers, in Japan the year before, Sergeant Morton had begun teaching me the ropes, not only weaponry and demolitions, but the stuff they don't, and can't, teach you in classes: how you go about being promoted, how the right word to the right person at the right time gets things done overnight that might take weeks otherwise. It's not really sneaky, though it can seem that way if you're outside the loop. Under Sergeant Morton's tutelage, I'd learned early to get inside the loop and stay there.

When Lieutenant Smith transferred out, while I was still in the hospital, Morton lost his regular drinking buddy, and I was a natural for the duty, except that I drank coffee straight. I came back from the hospital, and we talked more nearly like equals than we'd talked before, while mosquitoes dive-bombed us, and the lamp inside second platoon tent cast a yellow light that made the air smoky and dim.

Epps had nearly bought the farm, Morton said, when I asked how he'd wound up in my squad. He'd taken a field trip to Uijongbu, engaged a prostitute, and then refused to pay her. She yelled rape and the MPs arrested him. It turned out that she was under age and she had a firm witness to testify to her story. Epps was tossed into the division stockade, and the provost marshall initiated a general court-martial.

But the god that looks out for drunks and fools took care of Epps one more time. The day of court approached, and neither the girl nor her witness could be found. Instead of twenty years at Leavenworth, Epps lost his one stripe, for the third time, and got thirty days' K.P.

"But why'd you dump him on me?" I asked. "I can't imagine anyone I'd less like to have in my squad, except maybe Eleanor Roosevelt."

"Nobody thought you'd be back. Without a dedicated leader, first squad was a utility unit."

"He'll get somebody hurt the first time we go on patrol."

"I know, I know," Morton said. "I'll find a place for Epps. He's shipping out pretty soon, anyway."

We moved northeast, up the Chorwon valley, where independent units were assigned here or there as needed. By chance, first squad was almost always assigned to the 15th Regiment, building entrenched bunker positions and staring across no-man's land at the Chinese and North Koreans, who were building bunkers and staring back across no-man's land at us. We laid mine-fields in front of the entrenched positions to slow down their unpredictable night-time assaults, and we often did double-duty, standing night guard alongside the infantry, who could sleep during the daytime while we laid mines.

Epps got his papers for transfer to a construction specialist squad the second day we were there. "This has sneaky Kestner written all over it," he said.

"Let me see," I said, and he showed me the order. "Nah," I said. "See this line here? This order originated with Captain Kulbes."

"Right. That would be my guess, too. I was ready to request a transfer anyway." He edged closer, leaned his face into mine, and I tensed, ready to feint or dodge. I was up for anything, as long as he took the first punch.

"You're a good soldier," he said. "And you seem to be at home in the Army. I hate every minute of it. No hard feelings?" He offered his hand.

Epps had fooled me again. As he'd done before, he had pushed me to the point of rage and then backed suddenly away. Maybe Epps wasn't the problem. Maybe it was the chip I carried on my shoulder. I shook his hand and wished him "Good Luck", the last words I ever spoke to him. By the end of August, when the Chinese walked out on the peace talks, both he and Lieutenant Tunnicliffe had rotated out.

The war which had run back and forth from the Yalu River, in the north, to Pusan, at the extreme southern tip of the peninsula, became concentrated and focused around the 38th Parallel. The same amount of firepower was now spent on smaller and smaller areas, eventually to narrow in focus to single mountains, like Bloody Ridge, one of the more infamous hilltop battles..

In late August, similar battles would be fought all across the 38th Parallel for similarly meaningless real estate. Because of the new, limited scale of the war, the Chinese and North Koreans had time to fortify and re-arm, diminishing what had been our predictable superiority in mobile fire-power. The firepower that had formerly been spread across major fronts was now turned on smaller and smaller objectives, like a magnifying lens narrowing and focusing sunlight on ants. Casualties continued to be as high as in the larger-scale major offensives.

We laid thousands of mines in front of infantry positions, up and down the Chorwon valley. On night patrols, two of us would accompany the infantry, leading the way. Because there were so few with real combat experience, the duty fell upon a handful of us: Talley, me, and increasingly, Corporal Vandersteldt, who was proving to be attentive and quick.

Van was the son of a California dairy farmer, and he planned to start his own dairy farm when his enlistment was finished. He didn't drink or swear. He didn't run everybody ragged trying to get them saved, though he was a devoted Christian. It was as inevitable as gravity that, in time, we would talk about spirit and God and religion. I didn't have time for it right then, in the middle of a war and all, but I planned to get my coordinates worked out some time, probably when I retired.

Van had graduated first in his class at leadership school, and was soon assigned as my assistant squad leader. He was six-foot-seven and none of the guys in first squad wanted to share a fox hole with him because it had to be dug too deep, so, by default, he and I became fox hole buddies. We often worked around the clock, installing mine-fields during the day and then standing guard at night in two hour shifts, two men to a fox-hole, a fox-hole every fifty feet, in rain and sludge, emptying the hole of muddy water with an ammo box.

Somewhere down the line, firing would sound, and behind us, a mortar would thump. A flare would ignite overhead and parachute slowly to the ground, illuminating the field in front of us, hopefully, only on a probing patrol that would withdraw as soon as the flares illuminated them. The flares would burn out and the guns would go silent. We watched the darkness perched ankle-deep in mud. When it was dry, we served as supper to mosquitoes.

Early in September, we joined with the battalion engineers to build a road over a mountain that separated the Kumhwa supply route from the Chorwon supply route. Traffic between the two theatres of operation had to back-track all the way to Uijongbu, then repeat the distance on the other road. The mountain we had to cross was part of a finger-like extension of the central ranges: steep, rugged granite that, except for ox trails, had withstood human encroachment since the dinosaurs. Battalion engineers staked out a zig-zag route that led up the north side and down on the south, where we would meet A and B companies of the Engineers. We were given seven days to complete this assignment.

Amid sniper fire, first platoon hacked and shoveled, clearing a path. Second platoon was in charge of demolitions; Third platoon, on night shift, cleared and hauled away the tailings. We slept in pup tents and ate C-rations.

We used a forty-pound shape charge to open a hole in the rock. When that had blown clear, we cleaned it out with a fifteen pound charge, packed the hole with explosives, and set it off. We worked in overdrive, and just before dark on the fourth day, we met A and B companies about three-quarters of the way up their side of the mountain and ragged them about building a road for Christmas. They accused us of using a ton of explosives per ton of rock, but that was an exaggeration. Three-quarters of a ton is more like it.

Third platoon finished clearing the roadway that night, and on the morning of the fifth day we held a grand opening. Tom Ortega had brought up some red and white paint and we painted a sign on a large cliff face:

Welcome to Thunder Pass Summit
Courtesy of the Mongrels – Company D,
10th Combat Engineers

The first 2-1/2 ton truck passed over the summit and down the mountainside on what had to be the most crooked road ever constructed. It would jockey backwards and forwards a dozen times just to make the hairpin turns. We packed up and drove back northeast, to the company containment area, where we had a four-star mess, courtesy of the Mongrel cooks, and slept in our own cots for a night. This seemed elegant and lavish after pup tents and C-rations.

On the drive back, I had watched the farmers at harvest in their paddies. Stretched out in my cot after a hot meal, I saw them again in my memory and realized that I had missed the cotton harvest two years in a row. At the time, I probably would have said that I didn't miss it at all... wrestling dawn to dark with a twelve-foot sack while creeping down long, monotonous rows of cotton and the machine-like repetition of a few simple motions of grabbing and gathering and the isolation in all of it. Seeing the families at work in their fields and threshing yards was as sure a sign as the first north wind that winter was on its way. I missed that sense of connection to earth time.

A cotton farmer's year has a dozen seasons at least, all tuned to the condition and sensibility of the earth. There's a short fallow period, when the ground is frozen and inert and it seems like nothing could ever grow again and it's enough of a job to keep warm and fed. Then there are the spring plowings in preparation for planting. After planting, there are three or four weedings before the cotton is laid by, when you wait for the bolls to open and the plants themselves to begin to wither. Following that brief lull, harvest becomes a non-stop race against rain and insects and the market. Finally, there's a reckoning that comes each year, when you find out how you've done and measure the depth of your pocketbook against the length of the coming winter.

But there's an infinity about farm labor that corrodes any little conceit you might work up about its organic connectedness to the natural process of the planet. If you're seventeen years old, in the middle of a field, in the middle of the day, in the middle of the harvest, you look around at a million plants and know that each has to be picked...the natural inclination is to hurry down to the Army recruiter's office.

Natural time is a juggernaut that will crush you with its limitless capacity for dull repetition. Add that to a system of ownership that maintains a whole class of homeless, propertyless, hopeless farmworkers willing to work for chicken scratch and you get the share-cropping system that left my father poor, hungry and bound, each spring, to throw his aging body against the grudging bounty of the earth and the landlord.

The alarm sounded. First squad woke and dressed in the early dawn. We had a quick chow in the mess tent, loaded the pole trailer with Bounding Bettys, and drove north, to pick up a handful of Korean laborers. From there, we drove into the mountains where we met with an infantry squad. They led the way back up to a company of the "Can Do" 15th Regiment, on a ridge overlooking a small valley where the farmers had had to abandon their crops and their homes. A forest silence hung in the air, broken now and then by sniper fire.

I checked in with the infantry captain at the command post, and we walked the perimeter, getting a sense of the most likely spots for an attack. Van took charge of the laborers who would carry and unload mines while Talley, Bishop and I walked downhill, our boots sliding in the forest mulch, to begin laying out the field.

Bounding Bettys, or M-2A4's, are metal fragmentation mines that weigh five pounds, but only half-a-pound is explosive. They are activated either by direct pressure or by trip wires in an initial detonation that launches them into the air, where the second detonation occurs, spraying metal shrapnel at head and body height. They are laid in three overlapping rows, with trip wires criss-crossed between rows. According to the Geneva Convention, they must be mapped out and their locations recorded, for later removal. There is also required a strip of barbed wire fencing to mark the field.

Out in front of the trenches, we were easy targets. From across the valley there would come the crash of artillery, we would duck for cover, and a few seconds later there would come the answering roar from behind us. Their round would land, sending metal and dirt flying, and then our round would crash home across the valley. Then, silence.

We installed three different mine fields, eating as we worked, and finishing well past twilight. Since it wasn't smart to drive the narrow mountain roads at night, I checked in with the infantry captain and he assigned us a section of the perimeter. Nobody in first squad (including me) wanted to stand perimeter guard after a long day, but it was urgent to get the mines in the ground. Dinner was C-rations, standing in a trench, staring into forest darkness, waiting for the two hour shift to end.

About two in the morning, there came the screech of a highly amplified speaker and the brief rasp of a record needle. Then Frankie Laine belted out "Jezebel." All along the trenches, sleepy engineers and infantrymen woke up to listen.

The song ended, and we were introduced to Pyongyang Sue.
"Hello, Can Do Regiment!" her voice throbbed across the valley. "You can not do. You can not beat the people's army of North Korea.

"We are a friendly people, but we are determined to drive the aggressors from our land. This is not your country. Why are you here? Why have you come to Korea to die?

"This is not your fight. You have no right to be here. You should be home, with your wives and children and sweethearts. Why would you choose to die in Korea and make them sad?

"We have a very good solution. If you are tired and hungry and you don't want to die, step out of your foxhole and cross the line. Wave your handkerchief, and we will not harm you. We have food and showers and soft beds where you can relax and wait until the war is over. There is no need for you to die.

"You know that it is wrong for you to be here. This war is between the revolutionary peoples of North Korea and the capitalist puppets of South Korea. They are weak. We will overcome them, and we will overcome you.

"All the free peoples of Asia support our cause because it is just. Do not be puppets. Lay down your arms. Tell your leaders and your people and your President that you will fight no more.

"Now I play more music for you, your music, Johnnie Ray. 'Cry Me a River.' This is what your loved ones will do when they learn of your death."

Somewhere back there an artillery commander had worked out the coordinates of the speaker. Screaming Johnnie Ray began carrying on about some poor girl who had done him wrong and then realized that it was her big mistake. But Johnnie Ray wasn't having any of it. She could cry him a river.

There was time maybe for Johnnie Ray's girlfriend to cry him a pond, but not a whole river. The boom of a .105 Howitzer rudely interrupted. There followed the screeching whistle of the round overhead, the crash of the detonation, and the rest was silenced.

It was on nights like this, during the change of shifts, that Van and I would talk about God and man and law. I had tried reading the New Testament, starting from the first page, and gotten frustrated by the elaborate genealogies. Van said I didn't have to worry about that. First, I had to believe that Christ could redeem my life. I asked what that meant, and he said to make my life whole and meaningful, not just a bunch of events happening for who knows what reason.

I'd prayed my share of foxhole prayers, so I knew that I had some kind of belief in God. When Van and I talked, the mystery of my life became real again. There was no reason that I knew of that I had come through the ordeal of the Chosin alive, and I'd always wondered why John Grover had taken the rounds under the bridge instead of me. Then there was my burst appendix, and the Mori-Mori, going down on its first voyage after dropping me at Pusan.

I believed in something, I said, and Van said that was enough, to start with. I should try to remember, no matter what came up, that I was a child of God. He said I should begin learning to forgive the people I thought had harmed me.

"Even the Chinese," I pondered.

"They're doing their best," he said, "Just like us."

In the morning, we ate, loaded up, and drove back to Dog Company, sometimes to move out at once on a road assignment or another mine-laying detail. The worst assignment during this phase of the war was mine-removal. An infantry unit would relocate and we would be assigned to dismantle all the mines in the area.

It is not pleasant, removing mines. You have to approach each mine and insert a safety pin into a tiny slot before you dismantle the trip wires. If the firing pin is dirty or rusted it can go off as soon as you touch it. If the slot is clogged or the safety pin won't go in for any reason, you clear the area. You cover the mine with a half-pound of block of TNT, insert an electric detonator, back cautiously away, into a safe position, and set it off. Occasionally, one mine sets off another. Shrapnel whistles through the air. You wait for it to land, return to the mine field, check your map, and hope that the other mines are more agreeable.

This is about the time I got drafted into the Army. We'd returned to camp after spending several days on mine detail. With no assignment until the following morning, we bathed in the creek that ran past camp and tinkered around, repairing equipment and gear.

Fischer and Talley had driven D-21 back to the motor squad for an oil change and lube and fuel. I'd opened a new case of non-electric fuses and was testing them for burn times when Sergeant Morton came into the tent.

"Corporal Kestner," he said.

"Yeah, Sarge?"

"You're in a heap of trouble, kid"

"What is it?"

"The law is looking for you in Missouri."

"Why would the law be after me?"

"I don't know. The captain wants to see you right now."

I re-packed the fuses and we walked around to the command tent, Morton refusing to answer any of my questions. When we were in front of Captain Kulbes, he shuffled through some papers and selected several letters, which he held in his lap to read over. Finally, he looked up.

"Do you know the law is looking for you in Mississippi County?" he asked.

"No, sir."

"Do you want to tell us what you did back there that would cause the law to want to put you in jail?"

"Nothing, sir."

He looked again at the papers on his lap. "What I'm reading here tells me they are about to issue a warrant for your arrest."

"What for, sir?"

"Well, Corporal Kestner, it says right here that you failed to register for the draft on your eighteenth birthday."

"Sir, we were at Hungnam on my eighteenth birthday. Why would I register anyway, sir? I'm already in the Army."

"It doesn't say anything about that."

He managed to maintain his stern look another few seconds, then started laughing. "This is the damndest thing. You've been in combat all these months and here they are worried that you aren't registered. I'll take care of it."

"Thank you, sir."

"Here's what I'm going to say: I regret that Corporal Franklin D. R. Kestner did not report to the draft board within five days of his eighteenth birthday on December 21, 1950, inasmuch as he was under my command in the U. S. Army. We were aboard the U.S.S. General Freeman in the general withdrawal from the Chosin Reservoir."

"Thank you, sir."

"That should take care of it, don't you think?"

"It seems like it would, sir."

It didn't.

A week later, here comes the warrant for my arrest, courtesy of Mrs. Beck at the Mississippi County courthouse in Charleston. Captain Kulbes called me into the command post and passed me the letter. "You open this one," he said. "But I'll answer it for you."

"Let me answer this one," the First Sergeant said.

"That's fine," Captain Kulbes answered.

Now, Mrs. Beck was a notorious tyrant in Mississippi County. She'd run the draft board like the Spanish Inquisition all throughout World War II, and everybody had heard about her. In the backwoods, there were a lot of young men who failed to register for the draft because they'd never even heard about it. That excuse didn't fly with Mrs. Beck. Some of them didn't even know there was a war on. You can guess what Mrs. Beck thought of that one.

When I didn't register, she'd sent the reminder letter Captain Kulbes had shown me the week before. My mom had simply crossed out the address and forwarded it to Korea. When I hadn't reported in, the second letter informed me, Mrs. Beck had gone with the sheriff to my house to arrest me. Not believing my parents, who had told her that I was in Korea, she had issued a state-wide warrant for my immediate arrest. "Darn!" I said, when I'd read the letter and handed it to the captain. He scanned it and set it on his desk. "We'll get a letter off to this Mrs. Beck," he said. "Don't even think about it."

"Thank you, sir."

"Darn" was my favorite new word. Spending so much time with Van, I had stopped cursing, and was only beginning to relearn how to talk without using profanity. This isn't as easy as it sounds, since there aren't a lot of options in the the twentieth century. After you've said Golly, Gee, Gosh, Darn, and Dang a few times, you have to begin combining. So you try out Golly Gee or Gosh Darn or Gee Whillikers.

The nineteenth century developed non-profane swearing to an art form, but most of their words sound out of date. Gadzooks is a good old one, but it's one that fits only a few special occasions, mainly when you're thinking to yourself. Try it sometime. You can see the person you're talking to go away for a minute, brain on scan, trying to understand just what the fritz you mean.

"Zounds" is even older, from the fifteenth century at least, a blurring and shortening of "By his wounds" to "His wounds" to its final brief form. Nobody says zounds anymore. You hear "Cripes" now and then, and, once in a rare while, "criminy", but they're rarified and exotic.

One ends up inventing his own goshdang language. There was an older sergeant in first platoon who would occasionally say, "Sardine!" I tried that a few times, loudly and with great emphasis, but I could never quite get the feel for it, though I felt that the sergeant used it very effectively.

If you're in a name-calling contest, you're out of luck. "Son of a biscuit" is about it. In the European tradition, animals do the job. Son of a goat, or cow-face, or chicken head all render their message quite effectively, but they have an air of the self-conscious in American English.

Johnny Carson advanced the cause of non-profane swearing immeasurably, especially in the technique of exaggerating one quality of your opponent, like when he called Ed McMahon "Alimony Breath." But original language like that requires either a team of writers or lucky immediate inspiration. In Korea, I didn't have either, so I relied on a few stand-bys, especially "Darn"..

I became a sort of a hall-monitor when Van was around and somebody in first squad launched into a particularly blue outburst: "Stop your swearing," I'd say.

"Are we offending Reverend Vanderstilt?" became the standard rejoinder, and at about that level, I let it slide. Hell, I forgot myself, now and then.

But not swearing was only one of the symptoms of my developing friendship with Van, and probably not the most important one, at that. I was becoming a kinder and gentler Little Caesar, willing to listen a little longer, a little less cocksure that I was right all the time.

I never got mushy or anything, don't misunderstand me, and I never forgot what we were in Korea to do, but I did begin to practice patience and tolerance for others, even when they were wrong and I knew they were wrong. It was a major change for me. I'd grown up on the sidelines of the endless war my father fought with everyone, and I had learned early that tolerance wasn't in our vocabulary. In fact, when I was ten years old, my own rashness had closed down a church.

Chapter 15:

The Church of the Haunting

After the last chopping is done and the cotton has been laid by until picking time, each sweltering day in southeast Missouri lags along like a jail sentence. If you're ten years old, and broke, there's no chance to earn pocket money until September. Movies are crossed off your social calendar. There's always fishing in the Mississippi, exploring the T-fold forest, hoping to be kidnapped by river pirates, or to find a buried treasure trove, or a lost Indian tribe. You have duels with sticks. You have Indian wars. But at six or so, after a supper of biscuits and greens and catfish, you're sitting in the yard with the grown-ups, yawning and itching.

Daddy would hang a smoldering rag at the corner of the house to drive the mosquitoes away. All along share-cropper's row, families sat on door stoops, or carried kitchen chairs into the front yards, waiting for the cool of dark. Kids ran here and there in the dirt road.

It was exciting when the Revival began, in August, at the colored Pentecostal Church a mile or two away. Before and after meetings, the otherwise empty road would be filled with grown ups and kids, whites and negroes, walking and talking together, drawn perhaps as much for the pure movement as out of any deep spiritual hunger. They would congregate in the little yard of the church before and after meetings, their voices mingling like a natural sound, a brook in the forest or wind in the treetops.

We climbed trees to spy on them, Bob Raymond, Gaither Smith and I, sons of sharecroppers, bored nearly into comas by the turtle pace of summer. Now and then Slewfoot, who was my best friend, would show up, but most of the time, it was the three of us. Slew lived several miles from share-cropper row, in a housetrailer by the levee, and spent lots of nights fishing with his father.

For the first few nights of the revival, it was enough to watch and listen. The meetings always began in a song service with lots of energy, people dancing in the spirit and making the little wood-frame building shake. This was followed by an offering. Then Reverend Matthew Jefferson, who had heard the call in St. Louis to convert the backwoods heathens, would begin to preach, starting slowly, with a scripture reading, but as soon as he found his stride, he slammed into overdrive. Among a rapid fire of hallelulahs and Glorys and Amens, he would run up and down the aisle of the church, singing, preaching, patting his Bible for emphasis. There would follow a healing service and prayer call, and finally, the church would empty. People would chatter about the sermon while they walked back up the dark road to home and we followed them at a safe distance, like proper spies.

On about the third night of the revival, Gaither Smith noticed that there always came a time in his sermon when Reverend Jefferson would dance around the old King Heater at the back of the church and pray repeatedly for a sign.

"We need to help him out," Gaither said. "He sorely needs a sign."

"What did you have in mind?" Bob asked.

"I don't know. We should be able to think of something."

An idea came to me the next morning, and when I told Gaither, who lived across the road, on the colored-folk side of sharecropper row, he agreed that it was a fitting sign. We worked out the details with Slew and Bob and took an oath never to tell, no matter what, pricking a finger with a pin and dotting with blood a piece of Big Chief school paper beside our signatures. Next, we drew straws to see who would climb into the attic. It would mean hiding there in the hot afternoon, waiting with Old Tom, my grandfather's night-prowling cat, tied inside a tow sack, for the song service and most of the sermon to be over before we could deliver a sign. Gaither and I drew the short straws.

At four, we met outside the church. Gaither took the tow sack with Old Tom inside, and I carried the tin of High Life, a tarry turpentine that Grandpa used when he was training mules. Country doors were always left unlocked in those days, and we entered through the side door beside the pulpit, where Slew and Bob helped us up through a scuttle hole, then passed up the tow sack and the High Life.

Gaither and I crawled along the tops of the rafters, through cob webs and silty, fine dust that covered everything and floated into the air with the slightest movement, pulling the tow sack along behind us. When we got to the front of the building, we sat on opposite sides of the stove pipe and unscrewed the bolts with my grandfather's crescent wrench. With the bolts out, I lifted and twisted the old pipe out of place. It finally slipped loose at the top, and ten years' worth of soot rained down on me. Gaither laughed.

"Shhh," I said.

"You look like a negro," he said.

"Maybe, but it's not funny."

"Sure it is. Didn't anybody tell you it would rub off if you played with negroes?"

"You're the only one who said that."

"See? I was right."

The front doors opened, and somebody walked into the church. We shushed each other and stretched across the rafters, finding cracks in the ceiling to peak through. The church began to fill up, starting with Amen Corner and Deacon's Row.

When the church had filled, the minister offered a prayer, and Sister Robertson led the song service. Sweat rolled from my face and formed small wet circles in the dry dust of the attic. My back and my legs cramped up, but I didn't move. I could see only a small section of the church, the top of a bald head and a corner of a Bible held in the bald-headed man's lap.

The song service ended, and a Deacon led the congregation in "Shall We Gather at the River?" while the offering baskets went around. Finally, Reverend Jefferson took his position behind the pulpit and began his sermon.

"Our scripture for tonight is from Matthew 16, verses one through four," he began. He waited a moment until the congregation could find the verses in their Bibles, and then began to read: "The Pharisees also with the Sadducees came, and tempting desired him that he would shew them a sign from heaven. He answered and said unto them, When it is evening, ye say, it will be fair weather: for the sky is red. And in the morning, it will be foul weather for the sky is red and lowering. Oh, ye hypocrites, ye can discern the face of the sky; but can ye not discern the signs of the times? A wicked and adulterous generation seeketh after a sign; and there shall be no sign given unto it...."

There was a long silence. Finally, Reverend Jefferson began again to speak: "Brothers and Sisters," he said. "Let's not be like the Pharisees and Sadducees, pridefully reading the face of the sky and forgetting to read our own hearts."

"Amen!" echoed from someone in Deacon's Row.

"Now," the preacher continued. "We are farmers, and we have to read the sky to know about the weather. But we can't forget that the most important weather is the weather inside our souls...."

More Amens and some Glories... the sermon had its legs under it, and it changed pace in a hurry. Soon Reverend Jefferson was pacing across the front of the church, praising the inner weather that could discern the true prophets from the false, the word of God from the word of the world. Then he began to walk up and down the narrow aisle, his pace quickening, a new urgency in his voice replacing the tone of pleading with which he began.

Gaither and I nodded to one another, and he began to untie the top of the tow sack. I unscrewed the tin of High Life and shifted my legs so that Gaither had better access to the top of the stove pipe.

Reverend Jefferson began to run up and down the aisle, admonishing his congregation not to be, like the Sadducees, content with the surface of things but to push hard to the sweet marrow of the spirit. He approached the old King Heater and paused. "Lord," he prayed, "We ask you to show us how to turn from the false signs and prophets so that we can read the true signs of the times instead. Give us a sign!"

Gaither spread the top of the tow sack around the stove pipe, pushed Old Tom inside, and quickly pulled the sack away. When Old Tom scratched, trying to back out, I splashed the High Life onto his rear. He yowled and lunged, down the stove pipe, straight into the fire box of the King Heater, where he screamed and scratched from one side to the other and knocked off a lid which fell to the floor with a clang. Old Tom leaped onto the top of the heater in a black cloud of soot and ash, and leap-frogged across the backs of the pews, while the preacher and the congregation crowded out the front doors.

The church grew silent.

When we were sure that there was nobody still inside the church, we crawled across the rafters back to the scuttle hole and waited a minute for Slew and Bob, our trusty allies, to show up and help us down, but they had run away. We lowered ourselves through the opening and dropped to the floor. We ran into the trees outside the church grounds, where we knelt out of sight and watched.

The front doors of the church were flung wide, and the lamps inside continued to burn. Slew and Bob were nowhere around, there was nobody in the small front yard, and nobody on the road. Just a couple of Sadducees lurking in the forest surveying their evil work.

There were Indian burial mounds in the woods around the church, and the best general estimate came to be that the revival had provoked some unhappy spirit of the dead. Reverend Jefferson came in for his share of criticism as well. He was a city preacher who didn't know much about country matters and he was the one who had provoked the spirit with his endless harping about a sign. Signs were always all around you in the country, even if they weren't in the city.

Bob and Slew went into the attic a few days later and replaced the stove pipe, after the lamps had finally burned themselves out. The doors hung open for more than a week, and finally a deacon or somebody nailed them shut. But there was never another service held inside, and it came to be known as haunted.

Chapter 16:

PYONGYANG SUE

When I told Van about the church, I half-way expected that he would decide I was a puppet of Satan and beyond redemption. Nah, he told me, it just showed that I was a sinner, is all. All men were sinners, and the wages for sinning were our own deaths. That's why God had offered his son, to take the wages of death upon himself. Whoever accepted his sacrifice was free of the wages of death.

It was another of our night-time vigils; Van and I were talking in between two hour guard shifts while Pyongyang Sue commandeered the night, her voice broadcast from three or four speakers across no-man's land at about the decibel range of a jet taking off. From behind us, the artillery boomed, then stopped, while they plotted trajectories for their next shot. Except for the fact that she kept us awake, I kind of enjoyed Pyongyang Sue. Her propaganda was so obvious and so foreign to what I understood to be capitalist democracy that it seemed unnatural to me, and it seemed fair to listen to her blabbing in exchange for hearing the music of Nat King Kole, Patti Page, Frankie Laine. After hearing her only a few times, it was pretty clear that she played only songs that would awaken nostalgia and homesickness or romantic songs about betrayal and despair. But those were also the songs they were listening to back home.

I figured it was a not very well kept secret that most people were fascinated by death and loss, though they couldn't admit it very easily, and that made them sitting ducks for sad songs and sad movies and maybe even wars. One thing, you could listen to a done-me-wrong-song or you could read in the paper about the battles for Seoul, and imagine the pain of loss for a moment, maybe even feel, briefly, that instant reflex of nerves which monitors the whole body. As long as it was happening to somebody else, you could indulge that feeling for a moment, then set down the paper or turn off the radio, have a sip of coffee, and forget it.

Real loss isn't like that. There is no turning away, and there are no guidebooks for the actions you perform after that moment of natural self-monitoring. "OK," the brain tells you, "The stomach and lungs and heart are all ok. There's nothing to worry about." But there is something to worry about, and in war, it comes from where loss usually comes from, out there, beyond the limits of the mind and body.

Actually, Pyongyang Sue's propaganda may have been more effective than I thought. Here I was, ruminating on death like an undertaker. Like many people, I guess, I often overestimated my own thinking and underestimated the influence of others, especially when their opinion was repeated over and over, and Pyongyang Sue was nothing if not repetitious. The same sad few songs were played again and again and the same soft, feminine voice repeated how it was people like ourselves, farmers and the working class, that we were fighting against, and those at home who missed us were not politicians and statesmen, but people we loved.

Nat King Kole finished singing, "Mona Lisa," and the voice of Pyongyang Sue returned to seduce us, from the one remaining speaker: "Hello, No Can Do Regiment," she began. "Today, 300 American soldiers were captured in a battle north of Kumhwa. They are comfortable, now, and they want us to tell you that they are happy not to be killing innocent farmers and their families.

"I've noticed that you like to use the names of animals when you talk on the radio. Tigers and lions and bulldogs seem to be your favorites. We in North Korea wonder why you do not use the names of animals that are more suitable to you."

From behind us, there came the boom of a .105 howitzer, and the crackle of burnt air as it passed overhead.

"We have a list of animals for you to use," Pyongyang Sue continued. "Serpents, pigs, and hyenas fit you better for names than lions and..." there was an abrupt crash, the sprinkled whoosh of falling debris, and then, silence. I squatted in the trench and slept.

We remained on the line until noon the next day before we were released by the infantry captain and could return to Dog Company's bivouac. It had been a three-day assignment, and after early chow, first squad was free to turn in.

Next morning, I went into headquarters tent to read the bulletin board:

Notice: Effective September 2, 1951, Franklin D. R. Kestner is promoted from Corporal to Sergeant E-5. By Order of the Commander of the 10th Engineer Combat Battalion.

Seven ranks from private to Master Sergeant and I had five of them. My pay jumped to a hundred, twenty-two a month, though I never saw any of it, anyway. I'd arranged for fifty a month to be mailed home, and the rest was accumulating somewhere.

It wasn't a popular promotion with several of the older soldiers, and Morton said there'd been a lot of griping at the meeting when Captain Kulbes nominated me. The Captain had repeated that as long as he was in charge, promotions would be based on performance and not on age or length of service. It still didn't sit well.

I was assigned as Assistant Platoon Sergeant and moved out of first squad into the platoon headquarters tent. Van became the new leader of first squad. The transition required my full attention, and I didn't have time to get nostalgic about it.

Poor Fischer! Flossy wrote him explaining how with him being away and all, and she not knowing when he might return for sure, and what with Larry being so nice, they had married six weeks before, and she didn't know quite how to put it in a letter, which is why the letter was so late. So here goes Eusebius Fischer painting over her name on the hood of D-21, the third time it had happened to a driver in the first squad It was taken as scientific evidence that first squad was cursed as far as painting your girlfriend's name on the hood of the troop truck.

The war dragged on. Peking accused Washington of sabotaging the peace talks. Washington announced that Peking was playing politics with the lives of soldiers, each country seeking the high moral ground, and both appearing as frivolous and petulant as two bald men arguing over a comb.

Morale dropped, and General Van Fleet initiated a series of "limited objective" offenses, designed to take certain hilltops, Bloody Ridge among them. Second platoon was attached to our old friends in the "Can Do" 15th Regiment, west of the Iron Triangle, installing mine fields during the days and standing guard beside the infantry at night. There was still no replacement for Lieutenant Smith and with three squads to look out for, Sergeant Morton and I were kept busy, making sure that all the squads had enough ammunition, relaying orders from the infantry command, answering questions.

Van was proving to be a first rate squad leader, and first squad continued (in my unbiased opinion) to be the best in the platoon. I no longer had to stand two-hour shifts on guard duty, but I was on constant call, and got about as much sleep as before.

It was just twilight and most of the men of second platoon were sitting in groups inside their foxholes having C-rations. Northeast of us, the Air Force was on its last run of the day. We could hear the approach of the F-80 jets, the hammering of the Chinese .51 caliber machine guns and artillery, and the explosion of napalm and phosphorus bombs. The bomb explosions would light up the undersides of the scattered clouds between us.

There came the long screech of a jet going down, and we all turned to watch the darkening hilltops. The jet crossed a ridge held by the enemy and whistled down the valley toward us, trailing a black cloud. Even before he landed, there was the busy racking of .51 caliber fire from the ridge. We saw the puff of white against the dark sky as his parachute opened, about five hundred yards in front of our position. The plane passed overhead and down the valley, where it crashed, skidded, became air-borne, landed again and skidded in a slow spin to its final stop. The pilot released his parachute, and began to run toward our line, but fell in a heap after his first step.

It was darkening fast in the valley, but I thought I could see his shadow still crawling toward our position, and asked for two volunteers to go with me to see if he was alive and, if he was, to lead him back through the mine field.

Talley and Van came to my side immediately. When we had worked our way through the mine field, I could see that the pilot was alive and waving an arm in our direction.

The artillery began to pound the machine gun emplacements on the enemy held ridge, and tracers from the infantry .75mm recoilless rifles streaked overhead, silencing much of the enemy fire. Safely past the mine field, we double-timed out to the pilot, an Air Force Captain, who waved his arms more frantically the closer we approached, but seemed otherwise unable to move. A squad of Chinese approached from the forest, sprawled on the ground, and began firing at us.

"My leg's broken," the pilot said.

"I'll have to carry you," I said.

"I'll carry him," Van said. "You cover us and get us back home."

Talley took the pilot's pistol, and Van reached under his shoulders and lifted. The pilot groaned and seemed about to pass out. The enemy squad continued to advance. Talley and I returned fire and led the way back toward our positions, the pilot screaming with each step Van took. The 15th Infantry finally saw the Chinese squad and pelted their positions with .75mm rounds that effectively ended their target-shoot. Talley brought up rear guard while I guided Van, with the pilot in tow, through the mine field and back to our fox hole.

We set the pilot down and I called for medics on the infantry phone. The pilot's leg did a left turn about mid-way between his knee and his ankle, and the skin stretched white and bloodless over the end of the bone.

"It's a bad break, isn't it?" the pilot asked.

"Not so bad," I said. "It'll get you back home."

He twisted his mouth and tried to laugh. "I was going home anyway. This was my last damn flight. Ironic, huh?"

The medics arrived, and while they set about splinting the leg, the pilot reached into his breast pocket and produced a silk flag. (The flag is same as that on inside cover) "I won't need this anymore," he said and handed it to me. "Keep it as a souvenir."

On September 21, I was orphaned. Sgt. Morton got his orders to rotate back to the land of the Big PX. We sat up late in the headquarters tent, Morton slugging back some Seagram's VO in his farewell coffee.

"When I first saw you," he said, "I wondered what the Army was thinking, sending a kid into war, when they should have taken a strap to you and made you go back to school. But you've turned out ok, kid."

"Thanks, Sarge. It's mostly because of you that I've made it."

The wind blew through the tent.

"You know what?" Sarge said, after a minute. "I came into this war with a bang. I should go out with a bang, don't you think?" He tossed back some more 80 proof coffee.

"I think you're about to go out with a bang anyway, Sarge."

"I'm not drunk, Kestner. I never get drunk." It was about the first time he had called me by anything except Kid, though in his condition it came out Keshner....

"But you know what?" he asked. "Nobody gets next to me, but you sort of have." He sipped more coffee.

"You know something else?"

"No, Sarge."

"This is a rotten damn war. It's getting so all we do is kill people. It's like the trench wars in World War One." He saw my M-1 on the rack beneath my cot and pulled it out. "Keshner, is this thing loaded?"

"Yeah, Sarge, it's loaded. Be careful. It has a round in the chamber."

"You know you're not supposed to do that."

"Sergeant Morton, there are a lot of things you're not supposed to do. Do you have a round in the chamber of your carbine?"

"That's not the question. Whether there is a round in the chamber of your M-1 is the question." He slipped off the safety and squeezed the trigger. Wham! A large hole opened in the top of the tent.

"Doggone if it wasn't," he said. He slid the safety into position, took the clip out, and stuck the rifle under his cot. I turned over in my sleeping bag and fell fast asleep.

The tent flap opened about half a minute later, and Liutenant Taggert walked in. "What happened out here?" he asked. "I thought I heard a rifle shot."

"I didn't hear anything, Lieutenant," Morton answers, then turns to me, "Kestner, did you hear any rifle fire?"

I turn over in my cot and look at him: "Rifle what? I'm tired." I could see smoke rising from the muzzle of the M-1 on the rack under Morton's cot. The tent reeked of gun fire.

"Go back to sleep," the lieutenant said and quit the tent.

"Goodnight, Kestner," Sarge said.

"Goodnight, Sarge." I rolled over and closed my eyes. A minute passed.

"Kestner!" Morton whispers.

I try to ignore him.

"Kestner!" he repeats, pronouncing my name just right. The lieutenant's visit has sobered him up. He sits up and begins to shake me. "You get the tent kit out," he says. "We have to patch the tent. We'll patch both sides and by tomorrow morning it will be dry."

Since I was the light one, I was elected to climb the tent, in the darkness, and patch the topside, while Morton perched drunkenly on a tool kit set on end and held the canvas in place from the inside. When we had patched both sides, he walked outside to throw dirt onto the patch, trying to cover it but making it more obvious than ever.

Back inside, he asked for my rifle rod and ran an oiled patch through the barrel. Finally, a few hours before dawn, we went to sleep.

Next morning, the cook fixed him a special breakfast and carried it over himself. I had duties, but when I saw the replacement truck show up from division later that morning, I walked over to the tent.

"Franklin," Morton said, "I don't believe in goodbye. We'll meet somewhere down the road. You're a damned good soldier and you're going to make a fine NCO." I offered to take his bags.

"Nope." he said. "A soldier always carries his own bag."

When he'd been gone only a few minutes, High Pockets came in to the tent to see if Morton had maybe forgotten his whiskey.

"Don't be down in the mouth, Kestner," he said. "It was past time for Morton to get out of this war. It's time for me to get out of here, for that matter. Or they could promote me to general, and the war would be over in a hurry."

"High Pockets," I said, "you're a hard-headed hick from Alligator, Mississippi. The only things you know about are mud and reptiles. You for sure don't know how to run a war."

"Maybe not," he said. "But I know for sure that you're the only one who likes it. I'm going to talk to the Captain and see if we can't all go home and leave you to handle it."

"When you talk to him," I said, "see if you can get him to get me some good help for a change." And maybe, I thought to myself, just maybe, I'm getting a little tired of the war myself.

Chapter 17:

A Note About Infantry Tactics

Second platoon was assigned to the first battalion of the 15th, installing mine fields to secure a newly won hilltop perimeter that, later in the war, would come to be called Outpost Harry. I was walking here and there alongside the squad trucks, drinking a last cup of coffee, and checking with the men to make sure we had everything needed. I looked back toward the command post, and here comes Van with the Chaplain in tow.

"Hello, Sergeant Kestner," the Chaplain said, his right hand and arm outstretched. "And congratulations on your promotion."

"Morning, Chaplain. Thank you." I had been bumped to platoon sergeant after Morton shipped out. We shook hands.

"We're going to have a prayer," Van said. "We thought you might want to join us."

We bowed our heads, and the chaplain offered a quick, short prayer. I had sat in on services two weeks before, when an equipment maintenance day happened to fall on a Sunday, and like his prayer this morning, the chaplain had offered a brief sermon that helped me to understand some of the ideas Van and I talked about. My respect for him, as a man and as a minister, continued to rise.

The prayer over and the pole trailers loaded, I reported to our new lieutenant, and we drove to the jump-off spot in the foothills, where we picked up a dozen Korean civilian laborers, and continued up the ox-cart trail to the infantry battalion. It was our third day on the mine field, the largest we had ever installed, and I told the squad leaders that I wanted to finish that day. I told them to pass it on that we would almost certainly work until dark and then be commandeered by the infantry to stand guard in their defensive perimeter that night.

We pulled in to the infantry command post, and the lieutenant and I went to the command tent while the squad leaders mobilized the men to move the mines into position. After we had checked in with the infantry captain, I talked to a sergeant from Company C of the engineers, who had been working beside us the past several days, digging in and fortifying trenches.

He said they were about to wrap it up and get out, and we should try to do the same. The infantry was edgy, he said. He thought they were expecting a massed assault that night. If my platoon were still here, we would likely find ourselves manning a portion of the perimeter in a major fire fight.

I thanked him, but there was little I could do about it. The likelihood of an attack only made it that much more important to get the mines in place, and only a fool would try to hurry men who are setting mines. The last thing you want is a frustrated, jumpy engineer setting a detonator and trip wires into five pounds of shrapnel that doesn't recognize you from the enemy. So you walk through it, cool and calm, no worries, even if the last place you want to be when the sun goes down is inside the infantry perimeter.

But that's the way it worked.

It was nearly dark when we picked up and packed away our tools. The platoon found spots behind the infantry trenches to eat the last of their C-rations, and I walked back to the command post to talk to the infantry captain.

"Sir," I said.

"What is it Sergeant?"

"The mines are in place, but it's too dark for us to return to our company. I'll need to report in."

"That's fine," the Captain said.

The first sergeant tuned the radio in to Dog Company's frequency. "OK, Sergeant, you're ready," he said.

I took the microphone. "Bull Dog Six, Bull Dog Six. This is Dog Two. This is Dog Two. Over."

A few seconds passed. Then, Captain Kulbes' voice answered, "Dog Two. This is Bull Dog Six. Over."

"Bull Dog Six, Dog Two unable to return to your location. Request permission to remain at this location. Over."

"Dog Two, this is Bull Dog Six. Permission granted. Over."

"Bull Dog Six. This is Dog Two. Out."

I thanked the first sergeant and asked the captain if he could supply rations for the morning.

"Of course, Sergeant Kestner. Was that Captain Kulbes on the radio?"

"Yes, sir."

"Well, Sergeant, your reputation precedes you. We're glad

1st Squad on break after mine laying detail.

to have you Mongrels here with us. I'm going to assign you a platoon position. How does that sound?"

"Fine, sir. I prefer to keep my men together anyway."

"OK, Sergeant. We'll put you right in the middle, between A and B companies. The first sergeant will show you your sector and get you hooked up with phones. Ask your lieutenant to come up, will you?"

"He had to leave, sir. We're going to need ammo too."

"The sergeant will help you with that." He turned to the first sergeant. "I want a direct line with the Mongrels, ok? And make sure they have all the ammunition they need." The Captain looked at me again. "Our spotter planes have reported that there are troops massing in front of us. We're likely to see some action."

Nobody in the platoon was happy about the way things were turning out when I passed the word. We strung sound-activated phones along the trench linking the three squads. Van and I manned a command post in the center of our sector. Talley and the infantry sergeant strung the platoon phone to the infantry command post.

Endersbee's third squad went back to the trucks and brought up the BAR and the two thirty calibers with all the ammunition we had. Van and Talley and I walked back to the infantry command post for more ammunition, arriving during a meeting of platoon leaders.

"This is Sergeant Kestner, from Kulbes' Mongrels," the captain said. "He has a phone hook-up tonight to the command post, and he'll be Dog Two. That should confuse the enemy a little. When you hear Dog Two, it'll be Kestner's platoon." He pointed out our sector of the perimeter on a map inside the command tent.

"Sir," I said, "I'd like to pick up more ammunition if I could."

"Didn't the first sergeant get you ammo?"

"Well. A few boxes. We need more."

"How much more?"

"Ten boxes for the thirty calibers."

"Ten boxes?" he asked.

"Yes, sir, and I'd like to have at least three more bandoliers per man of M-1 ammunition."

"Sergeant," the captain said, "Didn't you bring any ammunition at all?"

"Yes, sir. But you've set me smack in the middle of your perimeter. I'm not very comfortable tonight."

He laughed. "Well, neither are we, Sergeant. We know something's up out there. But we don't know exactly what it is."

Back on the line, I sent down word to stand guard, two hours on and two off, and I better not find two men asleep at the same time. Then I walked the trenches, talking to the guys. After one of my rounds, Van asked why I was so fidgety. "Nothing seems right," I said.

"We're all dug in behind good cover," he answered. "We have plenty of ammunition, and good fields of fire. We can hold this line."

"I know," I said. "But let's do this. Let's man the trenches with grenades." I walked the trenches one more time, telling the men to dig out a shelf in the trench and line their grenades up for ready access.

A new private asked if we were going to get hit.

"I don't know," I said. "But we want to be ready."

The hours crept by, and early the next morning, about the time I had begun to hope that we might not see action after all, Chinese flares lit up the sky. I scanned the valley and could see a returning infantry patrol being fired on from the trees across from us. The platoon radio broadcast: "Dog Two.... Over."

"This is Dog Two," I answered.

"Dog Two, there's a friendly patrol coming into your sector. Be prepared, Dog Two."

"This is Dog Two. Roger."

I used the crank phone to alert the platoon: "Friendlies coming into Second Platoon sector. Hold your fire."

The returning patrol had taken three or four casualties. They hobbled into our line positions, and an infantry lieutenant asked for help to the command post. I assigned several men to help carry their wounded.

"Sergeant," the lieutenant said, "there's a heavy force moving toward your position." The Chinese flares had burned out by then and it was dark down inside the trench. He rolled out of the trench, stood up, and repeated himself "...a heavy force."

I got on the phone to the command post: "This is Dog Two, Dog Two."

"Dog Two, Report!"

"Friendlies have passed through," I said. "They report that there is a heavy concentration of enemy approaching my position. Over."

"Dog Two," the answer came. "Stand to. Maximum Alert."

I cranked up the platoon phone: "Dog Leaders," I said. "Stand to. Enemy approaching our position. Maximum Alert!"

Too soon, there came the sound of muffled troop movements from the valley in front of us. I picked up the phone to the command post:

"CP. This is Dog Two. Enemy directly in front of our position. Request flares!"

"Roger, Dog Two. Flares are on their way. Engage the enemy at your discretion."

The sixty millimeter mortars sounded. Flares burst overhead and began parachuting toward the ground, casting a wavering light over the valley in front of us.

It was like reading the news of your own death. Hundreds of Chinese infantry swarmed across the little valley toward our position. They had watched while we installed the mines and skirted them entirely. When the flares burst, the nearest soldiers were halted and forming up for a charge.

I cranked up the platoon phone: "This is Dog Leader to all Dogs! Stand by for an attack. Stand by. Do not fire until my command."

The Chinese were still partially concealed by the slope of the hill in front of us. I wanted them to reach the rise where they would be clear targets. I hung up the phone and told Van to walk the trench and make sure that none of the squad leaders got trigger-happy.

"Dog Two!" the Captain's voice came over the command post telephone. "Come in, Dog Two!"

"This is Dog Two. Come in."

"What are you waiting for, Dog Two?"

"This is Dog Two," I answered. "They're not open yet, sir."

"Dog Two, don't wait too long!"

"This is Dog Two. Request more flares."

"Flares on the way, Dog Two."

The light caught the Chinese in the last minute before a charge. I cranked up the platoon phone. "This is Dog Leader. When I fire, I want the platoon to open up with everything we've got, and I don't want anyone left standing. I will continue to request flares. Out." By now, the Chinese had approached to about a hundred yards.

I called for more flares, then aimed and fired at the same instant they began to charge. The new flares burst above us, the thirty caliber machine guns and the BAR rattled. Immediately, from all along the line, there came a storm of infantry fire. I called the command post:

"This is Dog Two. Request more flares and artillery fired for effect within predesignated zones."

No enemy soldier had approached to within fifty yards, and when the artillery began landing, they began to retreat. I called the command post:

"This is Dog Two. The enemy is retreating. Pursue with mortar fire. Request that you provide artillery on both sides of the mine field. Out."

The enemy was directed into the mine fields by the artillery, and the battle was over for us. I walked the trenches, checking on the guys. We hadn't taken a single casualty. The forward observers began to direct artillery against the retreating remnants. There seemed little likelihood of another assault that night, but none of the dogs felt like sleeping. "Good job," I told the men as I passed through the trenches.

"You're a cold-blooded sonofagun," Van said. "But you're effective."

At first light, I walked back to the infantry command post and talked to the executive officer. "Sir," I asked. "Is it possible to get my platoon relieved?"

"Sergeant," the lieutenant said. "You did some job last night."

"Thank you sir."

"We need platoon leaders like you."

"We had assaults like that at the Chosin, sir. I have a good platoon."

I was stopped on my way back to the line by a Master Sergeant: "Sergeant Kestner!" he yelled. "That was one hell of a show."

"Thank you. Tell me, why did you wait for me to engage?"

"We're not stupid, Sergeant."

"What do you mean?"

"Didn't you notice that you drew all the fire?"

"Ah!" The light went on. "That explains why nobody else was on the radio, doesn't it?"

"You got it, Sergeant."

"Tricky."

"You still did a good job," he said.

When the C-rations came around, I sent down word that we would take them with us to eat en route. We would also take as much ammunition as we had brought. I'd had enough of infantry tactics.

We reached Dog Company bivouac in time for lunch, and while the guys lined up at the mess truck, I reported in to the captain.

"How'd it go Sergeant Kestner?" he asked.

"Pretty well, sir. At least, I guess it did. We occupied a platoon position for the first battalion of the Fifteenth Infantry, and we got hit pretty hard last night. But second platoon stood its ground. We accomplished our mission, sir."

"I've already been told, Sergeant Kestner. I've already been told."

"I'm proud of my platoon sir. My platoon did well."

"I'm proud of them, too, Sergeant. Good job."

Chapter 18:

Bull Dog Six, Out!

Our new lieutenant had been assigned in mid-September, freshly commissioned out of the ROTC, and still not sure what he thought about Korea. He would show up for daily duty assignments, turn the platoon over to me, then spend most of his days at battalion headquarters. He may eventually have turned into a good officer, I don't know. He had stayed completely out of Sergeant Morton's way, and he stayed almost as completely out of mine.

We returned from a fairly routine mine installation. After dinner, I went back to the platoon tent to write a letter home and maybe turn in early.

I was numb. I had reported in to the first sergeant, but I hadn't seen Captain Kulbes in the command tent. I was at chow when I heard he had been transferred out.

Kulbes' Mongrels were no more.

I lay on my cot and reviewed the faces of all the Mongrels I could remember, starting from a year earlier, when I had been Morton's go-fer, a peach fuzz kid determined to crack this Army business. Most of those men had already gone, and now the captain, too, had left, leaving Cookus and Henley, in first platoon, Tom Ortega and me, in the third, as the only survivors of Chosin still in the company. Cookus, Henley and Ortega were already on short-time, I knew.

Odd that a fighting unit like ours would just dissemble like that. Maybe what was more odd was that we would have all come together at one time and place. If you set out to design a company command, you couldn't do better than what we had wound up with by chance of the draw. Captain Kulbes and Lieutenant Rosen had boot-strapped out of the enlisted ranks, and they never lost touch with their roots. Unshakeable Lieutenant Smith seemed to have been in the Army forever and to have lived through every possible combat situation. Lieutenant Tunnicliffe was a model junior officer, exuberant and attentive and a quick learner. And the platoon sergeants had been tough and wise, starting with Sergeant Morton, who would always define for me what it meant to be an Army sergeant.

High Pockets pulled the flap of the tent aside, peeked in, and seeing me, walked over to the cot next to mine, and sat down.

"You guys got back late," I said.

"Ahhh, the lieutenant got involved in some battalion politics or something. We almost missed chow."

"That would be the first time for you, wouldn't it?" I asked.

"That's funny coming from old Army chow Kestner....Are you in here moping around?"

"Nope."

"You can't lie to me, Kestner. We've racked up too many miles."

"Nah. I was just thinking about writing a letter home."

"Listen," High Pockets said, "the Captain wasn't sure which day he would be relieved and he didn't want to go around saying goodbye every day. He asked me to tell you to take care of yourself. He said he wasn't very good at goodbyes, but to tell you that you're a hell of a soldier and he'd see you again somewhere down the line."

I missed the captain, and I missed all the other Mongrels. Under their guidance and encouragement, I had matured. I guess it's called male-bonding nowadays, usually with a superior, condescending tone, as though the speaker, male or female, had managed to arrive at a sane, normal adulthood without any guidance or mentoring whatever, but had sprung, wholly formed and complete, out of God's mind, like Adam and Eve, or Aphrodite.

Psychologists call it the mirror stage. It requires only a second, when the fledgling identifies himself with the position of his model. In a healthy world that identification happens between father and son, and something similar happens with females too, so it's not really "male bonding", but human bonding.

Pity the person who never accomplishes bonding and drifts, unsure of who he is. On the farm you sometimes see a duck whose mother died before birth. Raised completely by humans, with no contact with his own species, he waddles around behind his owner like he thought he was a short, fat sergeant or something. Better to be a duck.

I was heartsick, but the war didn't slow down a minute. There continued to be bloody fights for hilltops, all waged within artillery range of the 38th Parallel. Any single hilltop was as meaningless as another except as bargaining chips when the peace talks resumed, if they ever resumed. A poll taken that month found that 67% of Americans considered the war in Korea "a totally useless war." Like Morton had said, it's a nasty war when all you do is kill people. Under Van's tutelage, I could see how important it was to forgive. My grudges against the Japanese and Chinese and North Koreans began to loosen. I wasn't quite ready to forgive, but without my rage as fuel, I was actually ready to ship when my time came.

Next morning, we were attached to a joint operation with the 15th Infantry and the 64th Heavy Tank Battalion in the hills west of Kumhwa. We were moving north as part of a major offensive across the whole front...dubbed Operation Commando. A few miles up the mountain road, in an area still behind the front, we found ourselves at the tail end of a stalled convoy of M-46 tanks.

I talked to the commander of the last tank and learned that the lead tank had hit a mine and lost a track. I told the men to take a break and and walked up with Talley to see what was going on. It was Charlie Williams' tank that had lost its track, and he was an unhappy sergeant right then.

"Hey, Kid," he said, when I approached. "This is all your fault. You should have cleared the damn road."

"Yeah, Sergeant," I said.

Talley and I searched the road out in front of the stalled tank and found a couple of Chinese box mines, which we disarmed. When we walked back, I saw a mine in the embankment beside the tank where the tankers were working on the track. "Sgt. Williams," I said, "tell your men not to move. There are mines right behind you."

One of the tankers hit the dirt, luckily missing any mine.

"They aren't going to explode unless you hit them," I said. I dismantled the first mine and Talley and I searched the brush for others, finding two more. I was crouched low over the last mine, ready to slide the triggering device free, when here comes a jeep with a 1st lieutenant from battalion in a cloud of dust, bouncing along the small trench toward us. But he didn't stop behind Charlie Williams' tank. Instead, he guns it and shoots across to the road to the other side and into the trench.

There was an explosion and I thought at first that the mine in my hand had gone off. Flying dirt and smoke surrounded and suffocated me. I looked up and saw the front half of the jeep tumbling onto the road and parts of bodies skidding in the dirt. The front half of the jeep stopped about fifty feet in front of the tank, and the body of the driver landed in a tree about fifty feet in front of the jeep at almost the same time.

Second platoon's new lieutenant drove up and parked. He walked up nearly to where I was dismantling the mine and asked why there were mines here?

"Don't come any closer, sir." I answered. "I don't know why there are mines here, but I'm going to get first squad up here and sweep the area before we go any further. We've just lost three people. The driver is hanging over there in that tree." I told Van, who was in the lieutenant's jeep, to bring first squad up front and to have 2nd and 3rd squads check both sides of the roadway all the way from the end of the convoy. The lieutenant walked back to the radio in his jeep and called in to report what had happened. This was a clear break-down of radio protocol, since the enemy was listening. First squad arrived, and we began to clear the road. The steering wheel of the jeep was still intact, and for some dumb reason I pushed it and the damned horn went off, startling the whole squad. We had to cut the tree down to get the body of the driver.

I led first squad on a visual reconnaisance up the road, and about fifty yards in front of the lead tank, a round passed, whistling, through our ranks and chunked into the embankment. We dove into the dirt simultaneously with the roar of Charlie Williams' 90 mm. cannon. I looked up the side of the hill and saw a dirt cloud with pieces of a rifle and an enemy sniper tumbling through the air while Charlie Williams' fifty caliber sprayed the side of the hill.

Two Chinese soldiers came scooting down the hill with their arms upraised, saying "Yankee Number One, No Shoot! No Shoot!" Talley and Fischer escorted them to the rear of the convoy to hold for the infantry.

Even after the medics had removed the bodies, the lieutenant sat, vacant, in the front passenger seat of his jeep, still in shock. I asked how he was doing and he said that headquarters had cancelled our mission. I said first squad should maintain tank patrol."The tanks can take care of themselves, can't they?" the lieutenant asked.

"You never know," I said. "There may be some more enemy up there with satchel charges. It's always good to have some infantry support."

Charlie Williams overheard us and walked over to the jeep. "I agree with Sgt. Kestner, sir," he said. "We can use a squad here until we get the track back on this tank."

"We'll just stay until the infantry arrives," I said.

The lieutenant agreed and signalled to his driver, and we watched them drive away. "Thanks," Sergeant Williams said. "I'd be a sitting duck out here by myself."

We organized several fire teams to stand guard on the closest hilltops. The tankers were having trouble with the track, and we wound up spending the night sleeping in pup tents with four-hour shifts on guard duty. In the morning, after a stand-up chow, I took a fire team ahead on a screening patrol.

We had made only a small march when we sighted a squad unit of Chinese soldiers who saw us at about the same millisecond. We beat a hasty withdrawal to the tanks and set up perimeter outposts until a company of the 15th Regiment arrived and we returned to Dog Company bivouac.

Two days later, the lieutenant invited me to drive with him in his jeep when we returned to the area, where we spent several days. He stayed back with a plotting board, mapping out the mine field, while Lafonte and I began setting the first mines. I walked over to the lieutenant.

"Sir, did you ever arm one of these mines?" I asked.

"No."

"Do you want to see how I do it?"

"No, Sergeant. Your reputation precedes you."

"What?"

"Oh, it's a good reputation. But setting mines is just not something I look forward to learning how to do."

I returned to the mine field, where Lafonte was bent closer to the ground than he needed to be, his face red, suppressing a laugh. "Setting mines is not something I look forward to learning how to do," he said, nearly under his breath, so that the lieutenant couldn't hear.

"Oh well," I said. It might even have been funny to think about a combat engineer who didn't know how to set a mine as long as you didn't think about the men who would be under his command.

But I was on short-time, and couldn't undertake the lieutenant's training. Like the first Autumn day, when you recognize for the first time that the season has changed without being able to explain exactly how you know, everything about the way I felt toward Korea had already changed by the time I recognized it. I was proud of my service there, but I was ready to leave.

Chapter 19:

THANKS TO MRS. ELEANOR

Within a week of Captain Kulbes' departure, High Pockets, Cookus, Henley and Ortega shipped out. Along with Warrant Officer Dalke, I was the last of the Chosin survivors, and a short-timer. I was reassigned as Non-Commissioned Officer In Charge. This was a fancy title for a make-do job designed by the new company commander to keep me out of combat. I sort of invented my duty, day by day, working with the First Sergeant or the Headquarters Sergeant or the Supply Sergeant, mapping out mine fields, filling and filing daily reports, or shifting personnel between units. Other times, I checked to be sure that all the latrines and garbage pits were dug, that the tools and tents were in good repair, that the men had squared away their areas.

We adopted a second Korean orphan, Dicky, who was twelve years old, and who spoke about a hundred English words. He and Johnny followed me around the containment area while I fussed with details. Lafonte nick-named us Sergeant Nit-Picker and the Baby-sans. One morning, the First Sergeant told me that battalion needed one man for a one-day detail.

"Will Ruckles do?" I asked. He was a minimum who shouldn't have been in Korea at all, a cook's helper's helper who couldn't be trusted to crack one egg at a time, but who might well drop and break every single egg in a carton. I was covering my tracks, trying to force the First Sergeant to approve Ruckles as a choice for the detail to battalion. This is called the logic of bureaucratic evasion, and it's as necessary a skill in an Army rear unit as a knowledge of weapons and tactics is in a line unit.

"He's a man, isn't he?" The First Sergeant asked.

The question was too complex to delve into on short notice.

"Yes, he's a man," I conceded.

Ruckles was assigned to battalion, and I putzed around the company area. One of my new duties was to taste-test the company chow as soon as it was ready. We would have our meals hot and fresh, chatting with Dicky or Johnny and the mess sergeant about this or that. There was time for a stroll afterwards, to help settle the digestion, maybe around to Supply to see what new project Leland Lipscomb and Ramon Cruz, the company carpenters, were up to, or out to the motor pool to chat with the Sergeant. Our personal war had ended when he attended the service where we laid old D-21 to rest and I told Captain Kulbes that we were ok with the new truck.

127

I was, in fact, fairly at peace with the world. Even Eleanor Roosevelt, I figured, was doing the best she knew how. I attended Sunday services even when Van, who was leading first squad, was away on assignment. The chaplain and I would have coffee afterwards and talk, much as Van and I had done during our foxhole conferences. It was benign, peaceful duty, a plum of an assignment. It bored me to tears, literally, those tears that spring into your eyes in the middle of a great, wide-mouthed yawn.

Ruckles returned that night from battalion even more sheepish than he had been when he left, which was remarkable. Sheepishness was his main survival technique. You could assign him to dig a trench, say, and even mark a lime outline on the ground, then walk away, feeling certain that you had explained the parameters of the task at hand, feeling some of the joy that teachers feel when the light goes on in a student's eyes, knowing that there has been a solid, almost measureable communication. As often as not, however, you would return an hour later to check up and find that the trench had been dug at a precise right angle to the lines you had marked, or ten feet away, in an area having no relationship whatever to the lines you had laid out.

"Whoa, Private Ruckles, why are digging here?" you might ask.

"I got it wrong, didn't I Sarge?" Ruckles would answer. "I'm really sorry. Will you show me again?"

Anyway, here's Ruckles at chow after his duty day at Battalion, concentrating on his dinner like a puppy who has just knocked over the garbage for the dozenth time and who looks up at you with great, unhappy eyes, knowing he's gotten it wrong one more time. I walked around to ask the First Sergeant what went wrong.

"He nearly killed a Colonel, is all. He was ok for a while. They had him policing the area, and then somebody made the mistake of having him clean the officer's latrine. He got mixed up, though, and used gasoline instead of diesel oil.

"He finished up ok, and the Colonel goes out to the two-seater and sits down. He's smoking and reading papers and without even thinking about it he opens the lid next to him and drops his cigarette inside. The explosion dismantles the latrine and throws the colonel through the door onto his face. The medics are treating him right now for a scorched butt."

"Are they going to charge Ruckles with anything?" I asked.

"No. When they asked him what happened, he tried to explain, and they caught on pretty quick that he had no business being in the Army."

A day or two after Ruckles' assault on the high command of the 10th Engineer Combat Battalion, the First Sergeant was transferred home, and we were assigned a replacement who felt his place was to call company formation in the morning and quickly return to his orderly room to do his morning reports the whole day long. Warrant Officer Dalke, who had come to Korea from Japan with the original Mongrels, shipped out, and was replaced by a W-2 hot dog who didn't much like me. In his words, I was "too damned young" to be a sergeant.

But there wasn't much that he did like. He was servile with the officers and uppity with the enlisted men. He would return their salutes with a sneer, a cigarette hanging from the corner of his mouth. He had several nicknames, Sloppy being the kindest of them. He was always in the orderly room, working, working, working on the company payroll. Division had sent him down to a lowly company to get "combat experience".

The peace talks were resumed, at Panmunjom, and quickly stale-mated again. November rolled in, and we got our first, quick snows. They distributed winter clothing for everybody in the company except me. Van and I talked in the evenings and promised to keep in touch.

And then it was all over.

I was helping Leland Lipscomb nail an entry ramp together when Johnnie ran around the tent and told me that I had to go home. I walked over to headquarters where the new First Sergeant gave me my orders and said the Captain wanted to see me before I left.

The Captain wished me the best. He had thought about promoting me to Master Sergeant and keeping me on so they could take advantage of my experience. But I had served more than my share of combat, he said, and he didn't think Battalion command would be too gung-ho about promoting an eighteen-year-old to Master Sergeant, anyway. I thanked him for all his kindness.

Johnny followed me, chattering, "I no see you again Sergeant. If you were grown, I could go home with you." I loaded my things into the replacement truck from division, and I headed south, waving goodbye to Johnny. It was winter in Korea, with snow already packed on the distant peaks, where a hot war was still going on. The valleys were cold and gray, with dirt streaked ice in the shaded corners of the rice paddies.

I stayed for two days at a replacement company south of Uijongbu, where a sergeant in a replacement company scolded me for packing so many weapons and explosives. "This is a no-combat zone," he said.

Vanderstildt in newly issued snow gear.

"A half-mile north of here it's not," I said. I didn't say anything about the bayonet I had in my boot.

Two days before Thanksgiving I took the freedom truck to Seoul and loaded out at Inchon onto the slowest ship in the Navy, taking four days en route to Sasebo. Thanksgiving came and went unobserved aboard ship. This was my second Thanksgiving in Korea without a Thanksgiving dinner.

At the replacement center at Sasebo, I was issued a new basic allowance of clothes with all my ribbons and rank and loaded with 4500 other combat soldiers onto a ship to San Francisco. With no duty of any kind, I spent the next seventeen days in the library or walking on deck. Not wanting to think about Korea yet, I had little else to think about, and I drifted.

I wasn't the only one. The poker games and bull sessions below decks were quieter coming home from the war than they had been going over. There were few fights, if any, and nobody that I knew of was thrown overboard. The war was behind us, like a big meal that we would be digesting for a long time.

Landfall sneaked up on us in the early hours of the morning of the seventeenth day, and my first view of the States in almost a year and a half was the foggy underside of the Golden Gate as we approached, then the city appeared out of the fog, growing slowly closer. Finally we steered into the Embarcadero, where there was a military band playing "Stars and Stripes Forever" and wives and kids, balloons, the smell of hot dogs and pop corn, yells, and whistles. Soldiers crowded the rails, searching the dock for familiar faces. One last, long tug from the ship horn, and we were tied secure while the gangplanks were lowered.

A dozen motorcycle cops made their way down the long dock, their sirens blazing and their red lights turned on. Cops on foot followed and cordoned off the waiting throng. An hour passed. Husbands located their waiting wives and waved, trying to make contact. Soldiers made sad faces at their girlfriends.

Another hour went by.

Finally we learned that we weren't going to be permitted to dock at San Francisco, after all. We were soldiers, which is to say undesireable. There was of course no schedule or provision for meals aboard ship.

More hours crept by and finally, late that afternoon, we were towed back into the bay and anchored near Alcatraz. Welcome home. They began off-loading us a bus-load at a time for transporting to Oakland. It was late the next day when I landed there and was led with a group of other non-coms between cordons of police to buses.

It was twilight. The lights in the skyscrapers were already coming on when I boarded my bus and found an open seat close to the front, next to a Sergeant First

Class from the MP corps. In the front row of seats were a Master Sergeant from the 187th Airborne, and two Master Sergeants from the 15th Infantry. Across the aisle were a couple of sergeants from the 25th Lightning Division.

"It's a whole bunch of Sergeants on this sorry-jack-ass-of-a-bus," my seatmate said. He was barrel-chested and stout, with a broad, big face and enormous hands. "I'm Lonnie Alchesay," he said, and folded my right hand in his like a golf ball in a first-baseman's mitt. "I'm from White River, Arizona...God's country."

"Frank Kestner," I said. "From Missouri. Land of river pirates and Presidents."

"What's the difference?" He smiled. "Tell me, Sergeant Kestner," Lonnie asked. "Did you ever get crapped on like this before?"

"I don't think I did," I said.

The driver boarded and pulled the door closed. "Hey, Driver!" shouted Airborne Sergeant Bowen, from his seat behind the driver, "You can just drop us at the nearest bar. And step on it!"

There was applause from the soldiers, and the driver had a minute there when he could have enlisted with us instead of against us, could have said yeah, it's a raw deal, and he would get us out of the damned city in a hurry and stop as soon as possible, could have treated us like men instead of truant schoolkids or convicts. Instead, he took the high road.

"I'm driving this bus," he began, and turned to face us from the center of the aisle like he was going to lecture us. He was met with groans and whistles. "There is a bathroom in the back of the bus," he said, "and we are not going to stop before Fort Ord. If you don't like it, you're fresh out of luck."

There were more cat-calls and whistles. Sergeant Alchesay said that he wasn't about to be ordered around by a damn bus driver, and motioned for me to let him out. We crossed the bay bridge and drove up Market Street, stopping every hundred yards for a traffic light or a trolley or another bus, and he walked slowly down the aisle toward the back, stopping to talk at each row of seats. He finally returned to the front of the bus, where he knelt in the aisle and talked to the sergeants in the front row.

He resumed his seat beside me, and leaned over to whisper. "We're going to commandeer the bus. We'll stop for a steak dinner and drinks. Then, when we're ready, we'll go on to Fort Ord. How does that sound, Sergeant?"

"It sounds like trouble."

"That's my nickname," he said.

He stepped back into the aisle and squatted beside the Airborne Sergeant in the front row, talking. When the bus stopped at a stop sign, he reached forward, turned off the ignition key, removed it, and put it in his pocket. The driver turned in his seat, yelled at him, and stood up. Sergeant Alchesay pushed him into the arms of the Airborne Sergeant, who held him while Sergeant Alchesay sat himself in the driver's seat and started the engine.

"Next stop, steak and brew!" he yelled.

"You're all going to be arrested," the driver yelled. "From now on," Sergeant Bowen said, "we're going to tell you how it's going to be. We are going to stop for dinner. You can even join us if you want."

"You're pirates," he said. "I'm not going to have anything to do with you."

He swung a weak punch. The sergeant sidestepped, grabbed his arm, twisted him onto the floor, bound his arms behind his back with his belt, and gagged him with his own handkerchief.

It took about nine seconds.

For the next ten or so blocks, Sergeant Alchesay didn't miss a single garbage can with the right front bumper of the bus. We finally left the city, turned onto the highway south, and cruised for maybe twenty minutes before the bus pulled over into the parking lot beneath a sign that read:

Sutter's Steak and Seafoood

Cocktail Lounge Curios

Open.

We drove around behind the restaurant, and stopped with a loud whoosh of the air brakes that sounded like a satisfied sigh. The infantry sergeants got down from the bus and went inside. Pretty soon the highway sign in front of the restaurant blinked off and the infantry sergeants walked back to the bus.

"This is your last chance," the Airborne Sergeant said to the bus driver. "Do you want to come inside with us and have dinner? Hell, I'll even pay."

The driver nodded his head violently, no.

They maneuvered him off the bus into the arms of the infantry sergeants, who carried him back to the luggage compartment. "We'll stand guard in fifteen minute shifts," Sergeant Alchesay said, "starting with Sergeant Kestner and me, and then working from the front to the back. You guys don't drink all the beer before our shift is over."

It was probably three hours before we assembled at the bus again, in a cold cloudy fog, laughing and singing, carrying six-packs, glad for the first time to be home. Sergeant Alchesay opened the luggage compartment and removed the handkerchief from the driver's mouth.

"You ready to cooperate, partner?" he asked.

"Not until everyone of you is in jail," the driver said. He was a bit of a slow learner.

Sergeant Alchesay tied the gag back into place, rolled him onto his side, and removed his wallet. He walked to the driver's seat of the bus, turned on an overhead light, and copied down all the information about the driver he could find, then returned the wallet to the driver's pocket, and slammed the compartment door closed.

"We'll go to Plan B," he said. "We'll drive down along the coast and stop somewhere dark and steep and throw him into the ocean. Then we'll call the police and say he fell while we were stopped to go to the bathroom."

I wasn't too happy about the plan, but I wasn't about to take on forty combat soldiers. We drove an hour or so, then stopped on a wet, windy cliff above the water, where we all got out to stretch our legs. The infantry sergeants opened the luggage compartment and rolled the driver out.

"Hey! It's a nice night for a drowning," Sergeant Alchesay said. The infantry sergeants lifted the driver and began to carry him around the bus toward the sound of the surf rolling thirty or so feet below. "Pshew!" the sergeant carrying the driver's feet said. "Somebody has messed his britches."

They set him down beside the front of the bus, and Sergeant Alchesay knelt beside him. "Maybe he's had a change of heart," he said, and removed the handkerchief.

The driver had been thinking, and he'd come up with an idea. He had a spare suit on the bus. He could clean up in the toilet, change, and drop us off a quarter of a mile or so from the main gate at Fort Ord. He could forget everything that happened.

"I don't know," Sergeant Alchesay said. "We've got it worked out pretty well right now."

"There are too many of you," the driver said. "Sooner or later somebody would tell."

"He may be right," the Airborne Sergeant said. "There's always some damned blabber mouth."

"I vote we just dump him," one of the infantry sergeants said.

"Listen," Sergeant Alchesay said. "Every one of us has your home address. If we let you go tonight, and then in a week or so we hear that you've talked to the police or something, one of us will visit you and you will cease to exist."

"Fair enough," the driver said.

"What do you guys think?" Sergeant Alchesay asked.

"Nah," the infantry sergeant said. "I don't trust him. Look how much trouble he's already caused us."

"We'll vote on it," Sergeant Alchesay said. "All those in favor of letting him go, say aye!"

The vote was carried.

At daylight, Sergeant Alchesay pulled off the road about 500 yards from the main gate. When we had unloaded our bags, he handed the keys to the driver, who jockeyed back and forth two or three times making his turn, and started back to San Francisco.

The Airborne Sergeant told us to wait while he walked down to the main gate and talked to the MPs. When he returned, he called us into formation, and we marched, crisp as an honor guard in our Class A uniforms, up to the main gate, singing out a version of Jody Cadences that he had composed for the occasion:

Sergeant: We've been gone to the Korean War!
Troops: We've been gone to the Korean War!
Sergeant: Now we're marching to Fort Ord.
Troops: Now we're marching to Fort Ord.
Sergeant: We've come back to the States, you know.
Troops: We've come back to the States, you know.
Sergeant: Hup, two, three, four, Hup-two-three-four.
Troops: Hup, hup, hup, two, three four.
Sergeant: They didn't like us in San Francisco.
Troops: They didn't like us in San Francisco.
Sergeant: We weren't fit to be there no more.
Troops: We weren't fit to be there no more.
Sergeant: Because we were fighting the Korean war.
Troops: Because we were fighting the Korean war.
Sergeant: Thanks to Mrs. Eleanor.
Troops: Thanks to Mrs. Eleanor.
Sergeant: Here's what happened while we were gone.
Troops: Here's what happened while we were gone.
Sergeant: Jody was playing around some more.
Troops: Jody was playing around some more.
Sergeant: Now we're back and we don't like it.
Troops: Your right, your right, your right!
Sergeant: What's gonna happen when we get home?
Troops: Jody better get his hat and gone.
Sergeant: Jody better get his hat and gone.
Troops: Jody better get his hat and gone.
Sergeant: Your right, your right, your right.
Troops: Jody better get his hat and gone.

I don't know what Sergeant Bowen told the MPs, but not only did they not stop us at the gate, they also held up traffic for us to pass through. We marched down the broad entry to headquarters, brassy as a company of generals with orders from the President of the United States.

Chapter 20:

What's Gonna Happen When We Get Home?

They were ready to process us out at Camp Stoneman. We were at Fort Ord. They weren't quite sure what to do with us, so we waited. Finally, the company commander told us that anybody with orders could leave immediately, but he would need to speak individually with the rest of us about assignments.

When he called me into his office that afternoon, I said I would like to go to an engineering unit. He looked through his paperwork and made several calls. At length, he found an opening with the 34th Engineer's Battalion at Fort Lewis, Washington, and, holding his hand over the speaker, asked me if that would do. I nodded, and he settled it on the phone, then wrote out my orders and told me to go to Finance to pick up my pay.

I called an aunt in Missouri, trying to find out where my parents were. She gave me the phone number of my aunt, Carrie, who lived in Lindsay, California. My parents were staying near her, in a town called Strathmore, she said when I called, and insisted that I go directly to her house. I waited in the line at Finance, and the first thing I asked the lady who finally helped me was how I would get to Lindsay, California.

"You go to the bus station and buy a ticket," she said.

"Ah," I thought, "I'm an Engineer Sergeant E-5. I can do that."

"How much money do you want?" she asked.

The question stumped me. I hadn't carried any money at all since a 3-day R&R in Sasebo, Japan, when I'd been advanced a hundred dollars in Army script and spent about twenty-five of it on cokes, hamburgers and a studio photograph to send home. I had started at seventy-five a month, with fifty a month going to my parents. I had also paid three dollars a month for an insurance policy. That left me twenty a month for...let's see...

"Ma'am?" I asked.

"Yes, Sergeant?"

"How much money do you think I'll need to go to Lindsay, California, for thirty days and then to Ft. Lewis, Washington? I have seventy-five already."

"How long is a string?" she asked.

"Ma'am?"

She laughed. "How much do you have coming?"

"I don't know."

"Well, we'll figure it out. You'll get travel rations of $1.05 per day while you're on leave. You'll get travel pay to Ft. Lewis of six cents a mile. That comes to two hundred and eleven dollars. How much pay did you draw in Korea?"

"A hundred dollars."

"And you still have seventy-five of that?"

"Yes, ma'am."

"You don't like to spend money, do you Sergeant?"

"Not really."

"Well, let's see," she said, "Your base pay as a sergeant with under two years' service is a hundred-twenty-two a month." She wrote the figures down. "Your base pay as a private was seventy-five a month, minus the allotment to your parents of fifty dollars a month, minus insurance. You were promoted in January, 1951, and your salary jumped to ninety-eight dollars. You were promoted again in September. Then there's overseas pay...." She moved her pencil up and down the columns.

"It comes to nine hundred, eighty-eight dollars in back pay," she said after a minute.

"How much?"

"Nine hundred, eighty eight dollars. Of course, you get your travel allowance of two-hundred and eleven dollars on top of that, and you can have a two-month advance of two hundred and forty-four dollars if you want."

Criminy.

"Just forget the advance pay, ok?"

"OK, Sergeant."

She counted out a stack of twenties, added a ten, a five, and four ones, and asked me to count it again, for myself. When I had finished, she smiled at me. "That should hold you for a month, don't you think?"

"Yes, ma'am. Thank you, ma'am."

It was more money than I had ever laid claim to in my life, a cash bundle that wouldn't fit inside my wallet and would give me a limp if I tried to hide it in my shoe. I hid the bundle inside a sock in the bottom of my duffel bag, then went to the PX and splurged on a leather travel bag that cost a buck, seventy-five.

Feeling class A all the way, I caught the bus to town, where I paid $7.35 for a ticket to Lindsey, which seemed outrageously high, then walked across the street to a drive-in and had a coke and two hamburgers while I waited. The world opened in front of me like a covenant.

Once we were on the road, the bus driver told me his nephew was in the signal corps at Seoul and asked me what the action was like there.

"It's behind the line. Pretty secure."

"Where were you stationed?"

"Here and there. I was at Seoul for a week or two. Well, I was actually at Yongdungpo, which is right next door."

"Did you see much action?" he asked.

"A little."

"What kind of action did you see?" he asked.

"I'm an engineer. We mainly worked on roads."

"That's lucky," he said. "Lots of guys aren't coming home."

"Nope."

I knew exactly why I didn't want to go blabbing about Korea. It was going to take years for me to come to terms with it myself, and I wasn't interested in entertaining the bus driver or anybody else by telling them what I thought they wanted to hear.

I hadn't called my aunt to tell her when I would arrive, and there was no military band waiting to greet me at Lindsay the next morning. There wasn't even a taxi at the bus station, so I asked how to get to my aunt's address, and learning it was only about ten blocks away, hoisted my bags and hoofed it.

She lived on a quiet little street of two and three-bedroom frame houses, with tall, silver-gray eucalyptus growing alongside the road and green arbor vitae in the yards. There was a Christmas tree in each of the picture windows, and wreaths on the front doors. Behind the neat little chain link fences, the lawns were straw-colored, almost the only apparent sign that it was winter.

A little squadron of boys home from school for Christmas vacation was playing war in the side yard next door to my aunt's house. They watched me set my bags down on her small front porch and knock on the door.

"She's not home," one of the kids yelled.

"Do you know where she is?" I asked.

"Mrs. Nelson knows," one of the boys answered, and a freckle-faced boy in a torn Roy Rogers t-shirt walked into the front yard. "I'm Jimmy," he said. "Want me to tell her?"

"Please."

He ran to the front door of the neighboring house and knocked. When Mrs. Nelson answered the door in an apron, Jimmy said there was a soldier next door, and pointed to me. Mrs. Nelson stepped onto the porch and looked over, still holding onto the opened screen door with her hand.

"Carrie will be right back," she said. "She asked me to make you comfortable, and I got caught up with my baking and forgot to watch for you. You're Franklin, aren't you?"

"Yes, ma'am."

Jimmy ran over and offered to carry my bag.

"Which one do you want to carry?"

"Let me see," he said, thinking really hard. "I'll carry the big one."

"It's about as tall as you are."

"That's alright. I can carry it."

"Thank you, anyway," I said. "A soldier always carries his own bag."

"Really?" he asked.

"Well, most of the time they do. Here, you take this one, ok?" I handed him the travel bag.

"I read about Korea in the newspaper," he said. "Is that where you were?"

"Now, Jimmy," Mrs. Nelson said. "You let Franklin come inside and rest up a minute before you pester him with a million questions, ok?"

"OK."

Mrs. Nelson showed me to a leather armchair in the living room and asked if I would like a glass of lemonade. "Carrie will be right back," she said.

"Lemonade would be nice." I pushed myself deep into the arm chair. "It's pretty warm, for Christmas."

"We don't get the seasons much. Sometimes, at Christmas especially, I miss them. Most of the time I don't, though." She laughed and said California had spoiled her. "You just make yourself comfortable, and I'll bring you that lemonade."

She returned with a tall glass of lemonade for each of us, and we chatted about the weather and California and Christmas. Pretty soon, Jimmy and two of his friends poked their faces against the screen door. "She's back!" they said. Mrs. Nelson and I walked into the front yard, where my aunt welcomed me with a big hug, then held me by the shoulders at arm's length to look me over. "If you aren't a sight!" she said.

"I'm glad you came home when you did," Mrs. Nelson said. "I was afraid my husband would find out I had this handsome soldier in for a lemonade and who knows what else."

I blushed, and they both laughed at me. "Well, you two just come on inside," my aunt said.

Mrs. Nelson said she better see to a cake she just put in the oven, but she was glad to meet me, and Merry Christmas! I carried my bags inside the house and leaned them against the wall in the living room.

"That sofa makes down into a bed," my aunt said. "It's pretty comfortable, and anyway, your parents don't have room for you where they're staying."

"I don't want to be any trouble," I said.

"No trouble at all. Paul is looking forward to talking with you, and the girls will want to show you off to all their friends." She stopped, and looked at me again. "You sure turned out," she said.

"Thank you."

"Here," she said, "give me one more hug, and I'll fix you something to eat." We hugged again, and I followed her into the kitchen, where I sat at a small kitchen table to talk while she fixed a chicken-salad sandwich, to "hold me over till dinner-time." There was an evergreen and pine-cone wreath on the table whose scent filled the room. She turned on a little radio on top of the refrigerator, and Nat King Cole sang "Mona Lisa," of all things.

My parents weren't doing too well, she said. My mama was a little sick, and their pickup was acting up again.

"What's wrong with mom?" I asked.

"Oh, it's her stomach, mainly, but it keeps her up nights, and then she works too hard."

"She's always had to work too hard."

"I know, I know," my aunt said. "We'll drive out there after dinner, ok? Right now, you just relax. You can have a shower after you eat and stretch out in the hammock on the back porch, and I'll make sure nobody bothers you until dinner-time."

Now. I could eat C-Rations my whole life if it came down to it and not bellyache once, and even better would be the meals prepared by the cooks in D Company, especially if I'd just dragged in reeking of cordite, dirt, and sweat after twenty-four hours' duty, but Aunt Carrie had been blessed by a battalion of angels as far as cooking goes.

After a shower and a quick nap that I didn't think I wanted or needed until I stretched out and began to swing in the hammock, I met my uncle and niece. We talked in the living room while Carrie prepared dinner, and I was already intoxicated by the rich fragrances coming from the kitchen when she called us into the dining room.

She had prepared a large roast with new potatoes and carrots and onions, fresh green beans, a romaine salad with hot-house tomatoes and yellow bell peppers, and home-made sesame rolls. Uncle Paul carved the roast into slices about as thick as my little finger, lightly crusted at the edges and almost pink in the center. The new potatoes, browned and crisp on the outside, broke apart easily under the pressure of a fork for sopping the rich juice of the roast. After raspberry sherbet balls in glass bowls for dessert, we had coffee in the living room, and sighed, content.

Aunt Carrie had about two sips of coffee, then went back into the kitchen to clean up. I asked if I could help and she said no, thanks, soldier. Uncle Paul said that he had always thought the Army would make a good career, and I agreed. He asked about my next assignment, and I told him that I was going to Ft. Lewis, Washington, after my Christmas leave.

My cousin wanted to know if I would like to double-date with her while I was on leave. I said it sounded like fun, but we would have to see. My younger cousin got bored in a hurry and went to her room to listen to music. In a few minutes, Aunt Carrie came from the kitchen with picnic plates stacked with roast beef and the fixings and announced that she was ready. My older cousin, who was going to church to work on a Christmas project, walked out to the driveway with us and waved goodbye as Paul backed his maroon Packard into the little street. We passed slowly through town, then headed south on a one-lane blacktop road, through mile after mile of cotton fields that made my back ache to see and smell.

We drove past the farmer's house, an island of bright lights and precise lawns, fences, and equipment sheds. About half a mile further, we turned off the main road and drove slowly down a narrow dirt trail, the headlights bouncing with each pothole.

There was a wide irrigation ditch on our left, and shoulder-high cotton plants on our right that swiped the car as we inched through. Finally, the road widened where an unmarked driveway led away to the right. "This is it," Aunt Carrie said.

Uncle Paul slowed and turned into the narrow driveway. In the headlights, we could see the two rows of shacks, white once, but streaked now with old dirt and daily neglect.

"They live in the second one, on the right," Carrie said, "and that's their pickup. I think they're home."

Paul parked the car and we got out, not much to say to one another. There were several front porch lights turned on that cast a weak yellow light almost horizontally along the road so that the potholes vanished into deep pools of shadow. Four or five kids were gathered under one of the porch lights, catching insects. The cotton fields grew right up to the back doors of the tiny houses.

We knocked and waited. "Just a minute," my dad said.

He opened the door and stood there a minute.

"Look who's home," Carrie said.

"I see," he said. "You might as well come in. Your Mama's been sick." He backed away from the door, and we stepped single-file into a single room with a bed along one side, where my mom sat with a pillow between her back and the wall.

"Frankie!" she said.

I sat on the edge of the bed and took all of it in: the oily kerosene reek of the camp stove used for cooking, the pallet on the floor where my younger brothers slept, the window screens torn from their frames and hanging from the windows, the one yellow light suspended from the ceiling in the middle of the room.

I turned my face away when I hugged my mother because I didn't want her to see my grief. She told me how handsome I was and I answered that she needed to get well so we could go out on a date.

Dad said the cotton was good in California. He could pick two or three hundred pounds a day, and except that his hands were giving him a little trouble now, he could probably pick four hundred pounds a day, I should try to join him unless the Army had spoiled me.

"I'll see," I said. "But I wouldn't miss it if I never even saw a cotton patch again."

"Yeah," he said. "You're a fancy soldier now. You don't need to do honest work anymore."

Aunt Carrie set the picnic plates of roast beef and fixings on the counter-top and walked over to sit beside me on the bed, where she patted my mom's hand and said that she was looking better since they talked that afternoon.

"I feel a little better," my mom said. "My stomach isn't acting up like it was."

Dad pulled a dinette chair into the middle of the room for my uncle Paul and seated himself at the table. "I need a new battery on that old pick up," he said. "I have to get a jump everytime we go anywhere."

Paul nodded, and asked how he was getting back and forth to work.

"Ah, the labor bus stops at the road," Dad said. "And you better be there, too, because they won't wait a minute."

"Do you have to go back to Korea?" my mom asked.

"Nope," I said. "I'm on leave for a while, then I'm going to Fort Lewis, Washington."

"I'm glad," she said. "I've been so worried about you over there. There's nothing in the newspapers about it but how many people were killed."

"You ought to be worried," my dad said. "You signed for him. If it was up to me, he'd still be home. Maybe he could even help out now and then."

"Kids always have to find their own way," Paul said. "I don't think Frank much wanted to be a farmer anyway."

"Well," my dad said. "It's a sorry pass things have come to when the best a farmer can do is be a hired killer."

"How far away is Washington?" my mom asked.

"I'm not sure... maybe a thousand miles?"

"That's about right," Uncle Paul said.

"Oh... as far as that?" Mom asked.

"We want you all to come to our house for Christmas," my aunt said. "I'm going to fix a ham and a turkey."

"I don't know about that," Dad said.

"Oh, John," Mom said. "Of course we're going. I don't even have a range to fix a turkey."

"Well, we'll see," Dad said.

"Listen," Carrie said. "I don't want to be a party-pooper or anything, but Paul has to get up early, and we still have to drive back."

"I really should get going," Paul agreed.

"Franklin has promised to stay with us for a few days," Carrie said. "So you can't have him back tonight, Alta."

"That's all right."

I leaned over the bed to hug her goodnight.

"Oh! You didn't even see your brothers yet."

"You tell them I said hello, ok, and I'll see them tomorrow."

Dad followed us to the door and stood there saying goodnight to the air.

Nobody had anything much to say on the drive back to town. I rolled down the rear window and leaned into the corner of the seat. Except in the war zones, I hadn't seen anything in Korea as sad as the conditions my parents took as their daily lot.

Chapter 21:

THE MORE THINGS CHANGE

"How much is rent around here?"

"Are you thinking about something for your mom and dad?" Uncle Paul asked.

"If my dad will let me."

"Well, it's a little high in Lindsay," Aunt Carrie said. "Maybe forty dollars a month for a three bedroom. It's cheaper in Strathmore. Have another cinnamon roll, Franklin."

"Thanks," I said. "I've already had my share. I'll have another cup of coffee, though."

"Strathmore is closer to work for your dad, anyway," Paul said. "And speaking of work, I'm going to be late if I don't hurry."

He poured a second cup of coffee from the electric percolator, and Carrie walked ahead of him into the living room, where she opened the front door for him. "Now you drive carefully with that cup of coffee," she said.

He gave her a kiss on the lips that was brief, but it made full-contact. "See you two tonight," he said.

Carrie walked back to the table and, still standing, drank a sip of coffee before she walked around the counter into the kitchen. "I'm going to fix you a real breakfast: ham and eggs and hot biscuits. When will your brother be here?"

"Any minute, I think. Where would we go to buy furniture?"

She set a carton of eggs on the counter and leaned into the refrigerator, looking for the ham. "New or used furniture?" she asked, and set the ham on the work counter.

"Used, I guess."

"There's a furniture store on the north end of town that's pretty good. We bought our refrigerator there for twenty dollars. They deliver, too. How do you want your eggs done?"

"Over medium."

"OK. And the next question is, how many do you want?"

"Two would be fine."

"How about three?"

"Three would be better."

"Four?"

"Perfect."

"What are you two going to do about lunch?"

"We'll eat hamburgers somewhere."

My brother drove up while I was sopping the last of the egg yolk with a biscuit, and Aunt Carrie insisted that he have breakfast. Before he'd finished, my cousin walked into the dining room, yawning and rubbing her eyes. She turned on the radio and asked what was for breakfast.

Bellies full, we walked out into a crisp morning, with frost still gathered in the shadows under the arbor vitae, and down the gravel driveway to my brother's red '39 Ford pickup. "Sharp!" I said.

"Well," he answered. "There are a couple of bad spots. I painted it myself." The engine started with the first turn of the ignition and hummed, tight and tuned. We cruised through Lindsay, dual mufflers fluttering.

"Hollywood mufflers," my brother said. "I get a discount on everything at the Ford dealership where I work." On the highway south, he goosed it to sixty-five to show me how she held the road. "I still have to buy new tires," he said, "or she would ride even smoother."

In Strathmore, we cruised the main drag, then drove the back streets looking for rental signs. Although I'd thought a three bedroom would be best, I liked this two bedroom about three blocks from the grocery store with a white-painted wood fence around the yard. The bedrooms were large, with lots of closet space, and the living room opened onto the kitchen with an area in between for dining. There was a separate garage, and room for a garden in the back yard. There was even a tire swing hanging from an elm tree. It cost twenty a month. I paid the landlord for three months right then, and he said he would turn on the electricity and gas that afternoon.

We drove out to the camp and found my mom feeling a little better. "Frankie got you a house," my brother said, "in Strathmore."

"But it's unfurnished," I said, "so you'll need to get dressed and go with us to pick out some furniture."

Well, the idea of going shopping was always good medicine for my mom, so pretty soon, here we are in Lindsay. My mom would say, "I sure like this sofa but it's pretty expensive." and I would say, "Nah, we can afford that...and these armchairs and this sofa that makes down into a bed...and those bunks for my brothers...and this dining table with the matching chairs."

I paid cash, and they said they could deliver everything late that afternoon. We had milkshakes and hamburgers at the Dairy Queen, then picked out sheets and pillows, new dishes and silverware and cooking pans, and still got back to the new house in Strathmore before the delivery truck.

When the furniture was set up and the beds were all crisp under new sheets and pillow cases and spreads, the three of us drove over to the grocery store and bought anything that looked good. We left my mom fixing dinner while we drove back to the camp to tell my dad. I still had a twenty and some ones in my wallet and most of the bundle in my duffel bag. But the hard part was still ahead of us.

They were doing just fine where they were, my dad said when we told him about the house in Strathmore. He'd be ready to rent his own house anyway in another week or so. Besides, he had made some good friends in the camp and thought he better just stay around here, where he had a ride to work, instead of moving into town where he'd have to burn up a ton of gas driving both ways.

I tried to think how Van would handle it, and I just let dad crackle and hiss like a dry wood fire that roars with a lot of heat at first but burns up all its fuel in a hurry. It would be better for Alta, he said, finally, and I agreed. Still, it was against all his principles to take a hand-out from his son.

I told him I just wanted to see him and mom comfortable.

It was past dark when we pulled into the driveway of the new house in Strathmore, the bed of the pickup loaded with their things. My two younger brothers, who had waved and yelled at every car we passed on the drive over, leaped into the yard as soon as the truck stopped and ran inside, saying, "neato!"

My dad toured the grounds like an English lord. He decided that they probably should have just gone on ahead and built a tool room behind the garage.

"That would have been better," I agreed. "But there's room for a big garden in the back yard," I said.

"Yeah," he said, "this yard is going to take a lot of extra work."

We went inside, and after a quick look through the rooms, he pronounced that the house was pretty small for the four of them and not worth twenty dollars a month at all and too far from the main street.

I agreed.

Still, it would do, for now.

We brought in their things from the truck while my little brothers ran through every room in the house, slamming doors and yelling, and then buzzed through the living room and out the front door.

"Don't slam the door," my mom yelled, too late. She set the table for five while she fried potatoes and steamed corn on the stove-top. "This new skillet sticks," she said, pushing at the sizzling potatoes with a spatula. She opened the oven door to check the meat loaf.

It was time for Plan B. "I think we should buy a new car," I said.

"The pickup just needs a little work, is all," Dad said. "Mainly a battery."

"And a new carburetor," my brother said. "Plus it burns oil, and it probably needs a ring and valve job. The tires are nearly bald, too."

"Frankie!" my little brothers ran in the front door. "Did you know there's a swing in the back yard?"

"Really?"

"Yeah. You can go real high too." They fell backwards onto the sofa and began kicking their legs in front of them.

"I think a car would be handy," Mom said. "It gets crowded with the four of us in that pickup."

"You two got it all worked out, haven't you?" Dad answered.

"Dinner's almost ready," Mom said. "You boys need to wash up." My little brothers raced toward the bathroom like the living room had just caught fire. Slam! went the bathroom door.

"I was thinking maybe I could take you to work tomorrow," I said. "Then I could drive over to Porterville in the pickup and see what kind of car we could get."

"Don't go pushing your weight around on me," Dad said.

"I'm not. I just have a little money right now. We could go ahead and get a car, I think."

"You two can just talk about it after dinner," Mom interrupted.

"I thought you would probably go to work with us," Dad said.

"Well. Not tomorrow, at least."

"Stop it, you two!" Mom said. "I don't want the first dinner in our new house spoiled by arguing."

She maneuvered us around the table like prisoners of war, shushing at anybody who brought up the subject of the new car. She apologized about the meal, but the new pots and pans weren't broken in yet. My brother and I argued that it was just right, but the meatloaf was a little over-cooked and the potatoes were burnt black in places. The corn was rich and toothy, though, dripping with melted butter and salt. She'd thought to test out a store-baked blueberry pie, which we had for dessert with vanilla ice cream she pulled from the freezer like a Las Vegas magician, while my little brothers ooohed.

After dinner, we cleaned the posts and put distilled water in the battery of dad's pickup, then jump charged it from my brother's truck. He said goodnights all around and I rode with him to the grocery store in Strathmore on his way home, more to talk than to save a three block's walk.

I called my aunt Carrie from a phone booth and told her about the change in the Kestner fortunes. She said she was so happy for Atta and the kids and reminded me that we were going to have Christmas dinner at her house. I asked if I could buy the turkey.

"It's already bought," she said.

"How about the ham?"

"You bring yourselves, ok, soldier? That's an order."

"Yes, Ma'am."

I walked back to the house with only the stars for light, a rich, nineteen year old man taking the air on his birthday. Mom had folded down the sofa and was making up my bed with new sheets when I returned.

"Is that you, Frankie?" one of my brothers yelled. I walked to their room and pushed the door open. "Aren't you guys supposed to be asleep?" I asked.

"Are you going to live with us?"

"For a while."

"We thought maybe you went back to Korea."

"Nope. I don't have to go back to Korea."

"Goodnight, Frankie."

"Goodnight."

I slept a dreamless sleep and woke early in the morning when the kitchen light snapped on. I watched as Mom turned on the gas burner under the coffee pot, sniffling and walking barefoot around the kitchen getting breakfast ready.

She was feeling a lot better, she said, but she thought it would be a good idea if she took it easy until after Christmas. The truck started, and I drove my dad and brothers to the grocery store where the labor bus stopped, then drove up to Lindsay and stopped at my aunt Carrie's to pick up my things. Well, she thought I should have a second breakfast so she could hear all about the new house.

Doubly fortified, I cruised up and down the main drags, strolling through car dealerships and jawing with the salesmen. The prices were shocking. A new Packard like the one my uncle Paul drove was going for $1995, and it was advertised as a "Cost Buster." Nobody wanted to offer anything for the Studebaker pickup at first, but one salesman finally said he thought he could go up to a hundred on a trade-in for a '48 Sedan that High Pockets wouldn't have wanted to work on.

I drove to Guthrie Ford where my brother worked, and walked along the back rows, where the older cars, the ones I could afford, were lurking. They looked fit enough, sitting immobile, but I figured that each one concealed its bad destiny beneath a new wax job and tire-black.

I went to the front of the lot where the 'fifties and later were parked. Most of them were going at from eleven to fourteen hundred. I sat in the driver's seat of a '50 Chevy Fleetwood four-door with a sun visor, whitewalls and radio. It had only eight thousand miles. The interior was like new, and there wasn't a dent on her. But the sticker price was eleven-ninety-five. Even if they gave me a hundred-fifty for dad's pickup, I would have to get an advance to pay for it. Then I would be broke again, with most of my leave still in front of me and Christmas presents still to buy.

I closed the door of the Chevy and walked into the showroom and sat in the driver's seat of a new '52 Mercury just to see how it felt behind the wheel. It felt about like I thought, a car for a real rich man, not a thirty-day imposter, like me.

I decided I would drive back along the two main streets of Porterville one more time to see if I had missed something. At that moment, a short, bald man with a pink scalp approached me from the sales office.

"Your brother works here in our service department, doesn't he?" he asked.

"Yes, sir," I answered. "But I was just looking. I can't afford a new Mercury."

"It's a nice car though, isn't it?" he asked.

"Yes, sir."

"What kind of car are you looking for?" he asked.

"A four-door family car." I pointed to the Studebaker pickup decomposing beside the road. "I want to trade that in."

He looked at it without flinching a muscle. I figured he must need glasses.

"Were you in Korea?" he asked.

"Yes, sir."

"Do you know where the Chorwon valley is?"

"I was there."

"That's where my son died. Sam Guthrie? He was a Corporal in the 15th infantry."

"I didn't know him. I'm sorry. I fought with the 15th, though."

"Anyway," he said. "Let's see if we can't drive you home in a car. You need a four-door?"

"That would be best," I said. "My two little brothers are going to be climbing in and out."

"Oh? It's not for you?"

"No, sir."

"How much of a monthly payment can you afford?"

I thought a minute. No more overseas pay, so my monthly salary would be a hundred, twenty-two, plain. Minus the fifty dollar allotment to my parents and the insurance and laundry: that left sixty-seven dollars a month. "I can pay thirty a month," I said.

"That doesn't seem like a lot."

"Some of my pay goes in an allotment to my parents."

"Let me go into my office a minute and run a few figures," he said.

I drifted here and there among the new cars. After a few minutes, a salesman walked out the side door of the office and out to the row of cars parked beside the street, where he removed all the sticker prices from the windows.

Mr. Guthrie returned. "I just talked to Mama, and she thinks we should take you to lunch. But we have time to pick out a car first." He opened the glass door for me. "Besides the pickup, do you have any money for a down payment?"

"A little," I said. "Five hundred dollars."

"That's good," he said. "Let me show you our better trade-ins." We walked outside and he led me along the row of cars parked beside the street. "I saw you looking at this '50 Chevy before you came in," he said.

"I can't afford that," I said.

"You don't even know what the price is."

"I saw your salesman remove the price. It was eleven-ninety-five before."

"Things change fast in this business," he said. "Now, I'll vouch for any one of the these cars in the front row. Is there another one here that you like better than the Fleetwood?"

"No, sir."

"Good. Let's go into the office. Mama should be just about ready for lunch by now."

We drove out of town to a steak place where I ordered a hamburger. We all ordered iced tea, and after the waitress left, Mrs. Guthrie pulled some photoes of Korea from her purse to show me. The landscape was familiar, but I didn't think I'd seen any of the places.

When the iced teas arrived, Mr. Guthrie took a long sip, cleared a spot on the table, took out his pen, and drew a line across the back of a contract. "How old are you?" he asked.

"Nineteen yesterday, sir."

"That's what I was afraid of. I can't sell you a car on credit. Could you increase your allotment to your parents by thirty dollars a month to cover the car payments and get your dad to sign for it?"

"Maybe," I said. "He's a little stubborn."

"Well," said Mr. Guthrie, "you give me two hundred down, and I'll give you two hundred trade-in on the Studebaker. That will leave twenty-four monthly payments of thirty dollars."

"You can't do business that way, sir."

"OK," he said. "I'll throw in the license plates and taxes and a full tank of gas." He laughed and turned to his wife. "He's a shrewd trader, isn't he, Mama?"

"That's not what I meant," I said. "You'll go out of business making deals like that."

"There's nothing that says we have to make a profit on every car we sell," Mrs. Guthrie said.

"How much is the truck worth?"

"I'll take care of that," Mr. Guthrie answered. "There's a buyer out there for everything." The waitress arrived with our salads, and he folded the contract up and handed it to his wife. "When we get back to the lot, we'll let mother draw up the paper work."

"I'm not sure my dad will sign."

"Is he at home, now?"

"No, he's working until tonight."

"You come by the lot at five. You can drive your new car out so he can see it, and I'll follow you and talk to him. We'll have the papers ready and maybe we can just wrap the deal up right there."

Maybe not.

I was too late to pick Dad up at the grocery store when he got off work, and each step he took walking home stoked his fire. I drove past the grocery store looking for him, then drove home and parked the car in the driveway beside the house, Mr. Guthrie following right behind me. My dad came out onto the porch before Mr. Guthrie had even gotten out of his car. "There's no point in looking at that car," he said.

"Daddy, just listen to Mr. Guthrie a minute, ok?"

Mr. Guthrie walked up to the porch. "I've made a deal with the sergeant already," he said. "He's good at a bargain, your son. He's going to have twenty-four monthly payments of thirty dollars and he'll just increase the allotment that he sends to you each month."

"Which allotment?" my dad asked.

"The fifty dollars, Dad."

"The Army pays that," he said.

"Yeah, but it comes out of my pay."

"Oh." It was hard news for him. "Well," he said, "you for sure aren't going to send us any more than you already do."

"Daddy, I only need you to sign the papers. If I could sign myself, I wouldn't even be here."

"That's right. You're not even an adult, and you for sure don't belong in the Army.

"But I am in the Army."

"Gentlemen!" Mr Guthrie laughed and made an exaggerated gesture like he was breaking up a fight. "There's nothing to argue about." He winked at me.

"Mr. Kestner," he said, and turned to address my father face-to-face. "Your son has horse-traded me into a corner, anyway. I don't stand to make a penny on this deal, and if you don't want to go along with it, it's fine with me."

"Daddy, will you just look at the car?" I asked.

"Sergeant Kestner," Mr. Guthrie said. "Would you mind driving the car back to Porterville?"

"Oh, John, it won't hurt you look at it." My mother had come to the door. "Hello Mr. Guthrie," she said. "Would you like a soda or some ice tea?"

"Evening, Mrs. Kestner. I think I better not, thank you. Mrs. Guthrie is holding dinner for me."

"It's a pretty car," Mom said.

"How does it run?" my dad asked.

"Take it around the block," Mr Guthrie said. "The keys are still in it, aren't they, Sergeant Kestner?"

"Yes, sir."

Well, I knew my dad was stubborn, not stupid. I figured he'd start off determined to find something wrong with the car, and pretty soon he would start to figure how much twenty-four payments of thirty dollars would come to. He would look around the deluxe interior, maybe turn on the radio and the heater, gun it a little, squeal to a stop, gun it to a faster start throwing gravel up under the fenders, slow quickly to his normal putt-putt, drive back to the driveway, idle a minute, get out slowly and say, "Maybe".

All he said when he returned was, "Bring me the papers and I'll sign." Mr. Guthrie walked to the hood of the car, unfolded the contract, and pointed out the lines where his signature should go.

Chapter 22:

MEALS, WHEELS AND DOLLAR BILLS

With only two shopping days until Christmas, my mom and I started rolling up miles in the Chevy, going back and forth between Strathmore, Lindsay and Porterville. We listened to the radio and jabbered, with me repeating to her every ten miles that I had lots of money for once and her job was to decide who should get what, and what size it should be.

On the 24th, my little brothers and I dropped her at Aunt Carrie's and did a bachelor run on which she was uninvited. In new jeans, shirts and tennis shoes (worn straight off the racks), we stopped shopping long enough for a gourmet lunch of hamburgers and milkshakes. Ah! I've always believed they need to work hamburgers and milkshakes into the lyrics of the National Anthem.

And that's how we cruised into Christmas Eve, spending money like we were born to it. I even bought work clothes and a new twelve-foot cotton sack. I had managed to shift the subject every time he brought it up, but I knew that dad was biding his time and that after Christmas, he would want me to prove that the Army hadn't spoiled me for work. I got an acid stomach every time I thought about that sack.

My brother drove up from Porterville on Christmas Eve, and we had a Christmas Eve dinner that featured a couple of fat stewing hens with home-made dumplings. Later, we sat around the living room and debated all the reasons we should open our presents tonight versus all the reasons we should wait until Christmas morning. Dad said you were supposed to wait until Christmas morning to open presents, and his vote counted as majority. Like the army..this wasn't a democracy.

My brothers and I had found a Philco radio in red plastic that would sit nicely on top of the refrigerator for mom and a house coat and slippers so she wouldn't have to walk around sniffling and cold while she fixed breakfast. She and I had bought underwear and pants and shirts for the boys, a non-present present if you were eight and ten, so they also got Hopalong Cassidy cap pistols with quick-draw holsters. I'd thought they should get Red Ryder B.B guns, but mom outvoted me. Dad opened his present last, a down-filled cold-weather jacket in blue with a fake fur collar that would pull up around his ears.

It was nice, he said, but it really wasn't his color.

"We saved the receipt," Mom said. "You can exchange it for one you like better."

It wasn't worth the trouble just for the color, he decided.

Christmas dinner was about what one could expect, knowing the way my Aunt Carrie cooked. Only a Christmas earlier, I had been southbound on the U.S.S. Freeman and had gone without anything at all to eat on Christmas except for some weiners and kraut that the cooks prepared just before midnight. That meal was half a world away from the turkey, ham, sweet potatoes, green beans, mashed potatoes with giblet gravy and dressing we put away that afternoon. We rested a while on the back porch, talking and watching the kids reinvent the rules for playing croquet. We proceeded to assault the apple, pumpkin and pecan pies.

It was dark on the drive home, mom and dad in the front seat, dad staring like a race driver over the steering wheel at the pavement hurtling toward him, though he was only chugging along at about thirty-five. My brothers and I were in the back seat singing "Hark the Hare-Lipped Angels Sing" for about the fifteenth time.

"Work tomorrow," Dad said. "Are you coming?"

"Not tomorrow, Dad. Maybe the next day."

"Well, I'll need the car."

"John, there's no need to work tomorrow," my mom said. "Why don't you wait and we can all go together the next day?"

"I have to work for a living."

Somehow, before we turned in that night, mom managed to nudge, suggest, plead, bargain, cajole, or wheedle dad into taking one more day off. But the morning after that, I was breaking in my new work clothes and dirtying up my new cotton sack. That's how I would have spent the rest of my Christmas leave except that most of the picking was over and we moved to the winter grapes, which I had never done before, but would choose any day over cotton, though you do cut up your fingers. Besides, nobody but a saint could avoid eating so many grapes that you didn't get the runs for a day or two. We were together, and it felt good not raiding the money sock in the bottom of the duffel bag every day. One Sunday, near the end of January, I picked up my bus ticket to Ft. Lewis. Mom got so sick that night we had to drive her to the hospital at Porterville. When he could see her, the doctor diagnosed her problem as gas and prescribed an antacid. Dad didn't think they should take time off from work, so next morning my brother drove me to Aunt Carrie's to say goodbye, and then to the station. We sat together on the one wooden bench next to a coke machine and I tried a couple of times to find a way to understand my dad, but there is no way to understand self-righteousness. It makes all its own rules and changes them whenever it chooses.

The subject of self-righteousness brings me, naturally, to the city of San Francisco, where I was faced next morning with a three hour layover between buses.

I almost became a local landmark in the restaurant, having coffee and coffee again, refusing to spend a dime more than I had to or to budge one step out the doors into a city I despised, and still do despise.

Years later, as a Captain on my way to Vietnam, I was forced to spend a few nights in hotels in the city and was met with the same universal lack of courtesy I met the first time I passed through, the only difference being that during the Vietnam war, people wore flowers and ragged clothes and smelled of patchouli.

"Where are you going?" the waitress asked, and refilled my coffee cup.

"Ft. Lewis, Washington."

"Don't you have any real clothes?" she asked.

I let it slide. Who cared what a ditz working the graveyard shift at the bus depot in San Francisco of all places says anyway? But an infantry Master Sergeant sitting in the middle of the counter did care.

"What do you mean by that crack?" he asked.

"All your toy soldier outfits. You all need a decoder ring from a box of Wheaties or something."

"These uniforms mean something," he said.

"Yeah, they mean you can't find your way to the men's department."

"No, they mean we're warriors, and not pasty-faced, frustrated San Franciscans who never heard the word, courtesy"

The volume had risen with each exchange.

The cook appeared at the other end of the counter, and the waitress walked away, but you could see she had lots more to say, and truthfully, I wanted to hear it. In a city noted by servicemen during three wars for its appalling lack of courtesy, she stands out in my memory as a kind of patron saint of San Francisco, a local genius of bad manners. The cook, who was less charmed than I, sent her into the kitchen and walked over with the coffee pot and an apology.

The Master Sergeant was on his way to Ft. Lewis, and we swapped Army lore and tradecraft during the next day and a half. I told him some of my experience with Kulbes' Mongrels in Korea and he said he already knew of Captain Kulbes' reputation from Fort Belvoir, Virginia. At Eugene, Oregon, and at Portland, Oregon, and at Olympia, Washington, we were greeted at the depot by women in USO units who served us coffee, sandwiches and cakes.

We arrived too late for assignments at Ft. Lewis and spent the first night at Headquarters. The Master Sergeant, who was joining the 34th Engineer Battalion as the Battalion Sergeant Major, did a little research, and after chow that first night, told me that I should ask for an assignment to C Company, where there were openings for NCO's.

At my interview with the commander of C Company, he told me he was just back from Korea himself. He said that he had read my record and wanted me in his unit. He knew of Captain Kulbes too, and he figured any man from Kulbes' unit would be a good soldier. I was assigned as second platoon sergeant.

"You want to go to school?" he asked.

"Yes sir. As often as I can. I'd like to start with the combat construction foreman course at Fort Belvoir."

"You got it. The first allocation that comes down, you go to school."

The war in Korea would continue until the summer of 1953, fought over insignificant hilltops within a few miles on the 38th Parallel, and finally end in a stale-mate. Like General MacArthur and most of the soldiers in Korea, I had wanted outrigfht victory. What we won instead was an uneasy armed truce that continues until now, on the threshold of the 50th anniversary of the war.

I had believed that if I tried hard enough, I could work out a resolution to the conflicts in my private life at least, but the closest I'd come to that kind of finality was in the hospital facing my own death. What I learned from my attempts to patch things up with my Dad and my family was that life was a balancing act between what I wanted and what I could have. I didn't forget what Van and I had talked about, though, and while I couldn't entirely let go of all my grudges, the more I practiced forgiveness and tolerance, the less power those grudges had over me.

I settled in quickly and comfortably to my non-combat duties at Ft. Lewis, and only several weeks later, I was assigned to construction school at Ft. Belvoir, Virginia. I picked up travel pay and tickets for a first class sleeper on the Great Northerner. On a cold gray morning, we pulled out of Tacoma and rolled slowly through the twisting Columbia River Gorge. We picked up a little speed crossing the snow packed Northern Plains, but it was a slow, wintry passage. Finaly, we crossed the Missouri and pulled into the great station at Chicago. After a brief layover, we continued east, past the steel mills and factories, the mighty rivers and rich farms of my homeland; what I had fought for, and would fight for again, in Vietnam. I had meals on white linen and money jingling in my pocket. I was young and mortal, and for the time being, all my wars were at a truce.

WAR DAWG EPILOGUE

Captain Kulbes' service in Korea lasted a little less than a year, from the landing at Wonsan until his reassignment from the Chorwon Valley. During that brief time, however, Company D of the 10th Combat Engineers was awarded two Presidential Unit Citations, four Korean Presidential Citations, a Meritorious Unit Citation, the Navy's Presidential Unit Citation, and the Luxembourg Cross of Honor and Military Merit. Captain Kulbes was also personally nominated twice for the Congressional Medal of Honor, once for his role in defense of the Chosin Reservoir and again for his commanding role in the defense of Wonju.

Major Kestner and other members of Kulbes' Mongrels have begun a bureaucratic paper chase to see that Captain Kulbes' long-overdue Medal of Honor for the defense of East Hill at the Chosin is finally awarded, hopefully before the fiftieth anniversary of the battle. Given the widespread American amnesia toward the war in Korea, such time-lags are all too common. The Mongrels still have not received the Luxembourg Cross of Honor and Military Merit, for instance, though it was awarded by the Luxembourg government to the State Department decades ago. Similarly, it was only in the spring of 1997, during the conferences in which we were working out the details of this book, that Major Kestner finally received a Purple Heart for combat injuries sustained at the Chosin Reservoir in November of 1950.

It's a notable paradox that the disregard for the war in Korea while it was being fought has been matched by a growing interest now, at the end of the century, and for good reasons. It was during the war in Korea that the basic form of the Cold War took shape. With the potential of nuclear warfare as a constant threat, military decisions were increasingly lifted from field commanders and made in public and private discussions between heads of state. It was America's most pronounced media war until that time, one in which public opinion directly influenced funding and manpower decisions by the President and the Congress...more so than had ever happened before. The grudging consent of the public and the resulting manpower and armament shortages almost certainly prolonged the conflict.

These factors also placed field commanders and foot soldiers in precarious jeopardy. In the crucial first few months of the war, military units were undermanned and underarmed. After peace talks were initiated in July, 1951, until the armistice on July 27, 1953, this war by committee was waged as a holding action without clear military objectives except to assure that neither side had an advantage in the peace negotiations. General MacArthur, and General Ridgway after him, were often forced into strategic compromises that conflicted with their own military appraisals.

From this distance, General MacArthur's willingness to carry the war into China, with the implicit acceptance of the use of atomic bombs which such a war would almost certainly require, seems rash and ill-advised. On the other hand, President Truman's unwillingness to budge on that issue calls for belated respect. As a strict condition of the cease-fire, Truman also insisted on the relese of more than 12,000 united Nations prisoners of war, approimately 3,500 of them American. Although he was attacked in the press for prolonging the war, his dogged persistence speaks of a willingness to make unpopular choices not always exhibited by politicians.

finally, for better and worse, the war in Korea initiated the long period of sustained US militarism and armed presence around the world. This is a fact of modern life so long in place that it seems natural to us now. Eighth Army, for example, continues to maintain a force of approximately 40,000 troops near the 38th parallel. By contrast, the Berlin Wall has long been dismantled. The 38th Parallel was the first symbol of a world divided into East and West, and it is still a living hazard.

The Pentagon has estimated that the war claimed 2.4 million military casualties. Of these, American dead numbered more than 54,000, with a total of 103,000 wounded. Military historian Clay Blair writes that, when civilian casualties are added to these, the war claimed a total "of about 4.4 million men, women, and children killed, murdered, wounded, or otherwise incapacitated."

The Mongrels who lived through the war have been almost uniformly prosperous. In the summer of 1953, young Sergeant Kestner returned to the Boot Heel section of Missouri. He began dating Treva Sutton, and they married that August. With luck and grace, they will celebrate their 50th anniversary in 2003, surrounded by a quiverful of proud children and grandchildren.

Major Kestner's active military career extended until 1971, when he received a medical retirement for injuries sustained in Vietnam. The Kestners, with wife Treva now at the helm, soon established a highly successful business in Tucson and Treva and Frank only recently retired for a second time.

Major Kestner's role as unofficial historian of the Mongrels dates from 1987 when he began advertising in Army Times to locate Dog Company veterans from the Korean War. He soon heard from Colonel Rosen, who had served until 1970 when he retired from the Army to form his own international consulting firm. Through Colonel Rosen, Major Kestner wrote to Bob Henley. After his service in Korea, Bob Henley returned to South Dakota and began a successful construction company which he continues to operate now, a half-century later.

It was November, 1988, that Major Kestner, Bob Henley, and Lieutenant Colonel Kulbes, all long retired from the Army, met at a Florida reunion of the Chosin Few. There, for the first time, Major Kestner admitted to having tossed a block of TNT into the honeyhole during the hot summer of 1951. As ironic fate would have it, the radio operator from the jeep with the Colonel who got sprayed, heard his confession. Major Kestner apologized and learned that the Colonel had assumed that Chinese artillery was responsible.

Lieutenant Colonel Kulbes retired from the Army in 1964. He began working as a consultant to the city of Las Cruces, New Mexico, on engineering projects, In time, he formed his own engineering consulting firm, working on the canal system in San Antonio, Texas, among other projects. He retired a second time to Winter Springs, Florida, but after a short time became, first City Commissioner, then Mayor. In 1995, he retired for a third time. He and Ruth, his wife of forty-four years, continue an active social life, which includes get togethers to watch rocket launchings from nearby Cape Kennedy.

Bob Henley had kept in touch with Ray Smith and Eugene Cookus, who each had prosperous careers after Korea. Ray Smith worked as a glass bottle maker and eventually became manager of a bottle making plant; Eugene Cookus completed graduate studies and became an instructor at Harvard, Nebraska Junior College. Then, through Eugene Cookus and Ray Smith, Major Kestner was placed in touch with Larry Lindgren, who had retired from a successful career in foundry casting. In March of 1997, Larry Lindgren and his wife, Joey, visited Major Kestner and Treva in Tucson.

In 1991, following publication of *"To the Last Man!" Kulbes' Mongrels in Korea, 1950*, Major Kestner visited his home town in Missouri and learned from a relative that High Pockets Wilkinson had telephoned. High Pockets had worked on the Interstate Highway System throughout the south. On retirement, he returned to take over the family farm in Alligator, Mississippi, with his wife of 43 years.

In 1989, Major Kestner and Cornelius Vandersteldt met at a reunion in Nebraska. Van's wife, Margaret, became friends with Treva. They met again at a 3rd Division reunion in San Francisco. During the Kestner's subsequent visit to the Vandersteldt's home in Pismo Beach, California, Cornelius Vandersteldt's heart stopped and he failed to recover.

In 1997, Thomas Ortega became the most recent Mongrel to be accounted for. Surfing the net, he found the address of Colonel Rosen. Thomas Ortega had returned home and married his childhood sweetheart, who had waited out the war for him.

The war in Korea has often been called a forgotten war. If so, it is the kind of forgetting that results from repression, not from insignificance. It is as unpleasant to look at the calculated savagery of the war as it is unpleasant to consider its dollar costs. As in all wars, these costs were concealed in the national debt and continue until now, in the expense of maintaining an armed military presence along the 38th Parallel.

Psychology dictates that what we repress does not vanish but returns and is manifested in new symptoms. Korea was only one symptom in what is the underlying disease of the twentieth century. This disease has been described by philosopher Martin Heidegger as resulting from humankind's sudden technological and scientific dominion over the earth. Dominion carries the responsibility of replenishment, and we may not yet have learned the qualities of character required of such responsibility.

The Christian forgiveness that Major Kestner and Cornelius Vandersteldt began to explore during their foxhole conversations relinquishes vengeful domination in favor of a caring stewardship. Some similar sacrifice of the impulse toward domination in favor of replenishment will undoubtedly be required if the earth and its creatures, including humans, are to survive. Otherwise, the lessons offered by the twentieth century's epidemic of global devastation may remain repressed and unlearned.

Recently, North Koreans who chose to remain in South Korea after the ceasefire have begun to buy and import soil from North Korea so that they can be buried in the native earth of their homeland. This book wants to be, like that imported Korean soil, a way to remember and finally come to peace about a war which can't be forgotten.

-James Livingston

ACKNOWLEDGMENTS

The following books have been helpful in reconstructing troop movements and chronologies: Korea, The Forgotten War, by Clay Blair. (NY, NY: Times Books, 1987) Third Division in Korea, edited by Captain Max W. Dolcater of the Third Infantry Division. (Tokyo: Toppan Printing Company, 1953)

www.ingramcontent.com/pod-product-compliance
Lightning Source LLC
Chambersburg PA
CBHW060801100426
42813CB00004B/904